Rivers

Diary of a Blind
Alaska Racing Sled Dog

Mike Dillingham

Publications *Since 1978*
Consultants

PO Box 221974 Anchorage, Alaska 99522-1974

ISBN 1-888125-89-6

Library of Congress Catalog Card Number: 2001097701

Manufactured in the United States of America.

Dedication

To my wife Mary, who tolerated this entire adventure. She, like a true champion, took all of the ribbing about her "husband sleeping with the dogs."

To those who are confronted with challenges, strive to overcome those challenges, and achieve their true potential. You are an inspiration to us all.

Acknowledgments

Our dog Sandy, who had her back yard reorganized, her life changed, and felt a little neglected. She acted as a "guide dog" for Rivers. Yes, her entire world was turned upside down. Nevertheless, before Rivers left our home to return to the country, Sandy kissed him on the nose, and then growled when he tried to return the gesture. Truly a grand old lady!

Dr. Jim (Dr. James Gaarder DVM/DACVO), whose caring and skill resulted in Rivers becoming pain free and returning him to a quality of life long absent.

Raymie Redington, who let me work with Rivers and his buddies. Raymie answered all of my questions, while teaching me a lot about dogs and mushing. Raymie opened the door to another great adventure in my life!

My friend Ray, who will get upset if I say any more than "thanks."

Next are Linda and Kerry at the Blind Dogs web site, http://www.blinddogs.com and e-group, plus Jacki at IMOM who made the fund-raiser happen and a success. Linda also developed this web site, http://www.blinddogs.com/rivers.htm for Rivers.

Finally, a very special thanks to all of the people who donated either money or their prayers for Rivers' operation and recovery.

In memory of Rex and Tarzan, my friends, and canine veterans of the trail. And also Linda, a true champion.

7

Cast of Characters

Raymie, Rivers, and Mike

Lakota

Brownie

Christmas

Terror

Spot

Tip   Nitro

Sandy

Junior

Teacher

Doc

Ugly

Table of Content

Foreword

Rivers is a real live dog, a blind dog, a racing sled dog. Rivers was not born blind. He lost his sight due to glaucoma and cataracts. His sight could not be saved. He participated in numerous long and short distance races after he became blind because he wanted to. Rivers now lives with my wife, Mary, and me.

Why did I get involved with Rivers? Simple. It was because of his courage and his heart. He could have given up, but he did not. He is an inspiration to me. People who know of Rivers, or have read about him, tell me his story has motivated them to deal with their challenges and succeed. Frankly, working with Rivers and the rest of his buddies has changed my life for the good. I hope that *Rivers, Diary of a Blind Alaska Racing Sled Dog* changes your life also.

Thanks

Mike

Please visit our website at www.riversbooks.com
or contact Rivers at rivers@riversbooks.com.

Introduction

My name is Rivers and I am a blind racing sled dog. I have been blind for more than three years. During that time, I have raced the big sled dog race from Anchorage to Nome twice. I am almost five years old.

One day a while back, I was by my doghouse when I heard a strange car drive up the driveway. I heard my owner, Mr. Raymie call out saying, "Hi Mike and Mary. Come on in." Then I heard the man's voice with a funny accent say, "Hi Raymie, mind if I give some biscuits to your dogs?"

"Sure," Mr. Raymie said, "Go ahead. They are always happy to see you."

I heard my buddies start to howl and bark because they must of saw this man coming toward them. My buddies live a little down the hill from me, except for my best friend Lakota. He lives next to me and helps me "see" by acting as my eyes.

It was chilly and rainy so I started to go back to my doghouse. It is always the same; no one ever visits me. I seldom meet any humans. I hear people and I know they are visiting the other dogs, but they never visit me, or come by my doghouse. Sure, sometimes my buddies visit with me, but I can't play with them because I can't see. I guess I am no fun because my eyes hurt so much that I am seldom in a good mood. No, I never cry out, but my eyes do hurt all the time. I hear the other dogs having a good time. I wish I could join them.

Lakota is a very shy and timid dog. Although he is a very big dog, many of the other dogs think Lakota is slow because he is shy, quite, and timid. However, I know better. He is very smart and a good friend. He talks to me all of the time and describes the things that are around us

I guess I was standing by my doghouse "looking" down the road when I heard the man say, "Hey Raymie, who is that dog on the hill with the big eyes?

"Mike," Mr. Raymie said, "He is blind and ran the big race two times while being blind."

Mike said "That is amazing. Mind if I give him a biscuit."

I guess Mr. Raymie said it was okay because I heard footsteps coming my way and then I sensed a hand in front of my nose with a biscuit. I took the biscuit from Mike's hand very gently. The biscuit tasted very good. "Hey buddy, want another one?" Mike asked. I looked up toward the direction of his voice and smelled the biscuit right in front of my nose. I gently took the biscuit and dropped it where I knew Lakota could get it. I knew he would enjoy it. "Raymie, did you see that? He gave the biscuit to this other dog! I never saw a dog do that before." Mike said.

Mr. Raymie answered, "That dog's name is Lakota. He is very shy and timid. I keep him with the blind dog since they get along so well." As Mr. Raymie was talking, Mike rubbed my ears and my back. Wow! That felt good.

Mike gave both Lakota and me another biscuit. As I was eating it, I heard Mike and Mr. Raymie talk about my eyes. Mike thought I could see and asked if he could take me to an eye doctor for dogs. Mr. Raymie said he would appreciate that. He said he really liked me and wishes I could see; maybe some laser surgery would work. I am not sure what they were talking about, but I felt very comfortable around this human named Mike. Moreover, I like it when he rubs my ears.

They agreed that Mike would talk to the eye doctor and then see what happens. The next thing I know, Mike puts his hands on both sides of my head and puts his nose right in front of my face, and whispers, "A champion like you deserves another chance, buddy. Let me see what I can do for you." It felt so good to hear his nice words, while he was gently rubbing the sides of my head. Then I heard him walk over to Lakota. I knew Lakota would shy away from Mike so I told Lakota that he was okay and let Mike rub his ears. Lakota told me that he liked the ear rubs a lot.

Well that is how it all began. A chance meeting on a rainy

afternoon that started an adventure for a blind dog, and a human. Since I can't tell time and don't know day from night, Mike helped me write this story and in some places he wrote it for me. It is my diary or log of this adventure. I hope you enjoy it.

Take care - Rivers.

The Start

I understand that after I met Mike he wrote to many of his friends about me. However, I also understand that Mike's hearing is very bad and he did not get my name right. I think he called me Noble. Nice name, but my name is Rivers. He can't hear and I can't see! What a team we make! I heard Mike joke with one of his friends that I was his hearing aid dog, and he was my seeing eye human.

Mike took me to the eye vet because my eyeballs were so big. Frankly, I was in pain, but you know us dogs; we seldom let our human companions know when we hurt. Mike wanted to know if there was some way that I could see again. After a very thorough exam, Dr. Jim said that my sight was gone for good. However, the important thing now was to make me comfortable and pain free.

A long time ago, I accepted the fact that I was blind and there was no chance I would ever see again. But, I want to run races again. Mike knows I wanted to race, and he asked Dr. Jim if I could. Dr. Jim said there is no reason why I couldn't race again. Dr Jim knew of several dogs, also blind, that he has helped to race or hunt with their human companions. However, Dr. Jim recommended removing my bad eyeballs so that I would be totally pain free. Today, after the exam, I ran with Lakota and my other teammates for the first time in over a year. I was so happy to do that. I want to do it, and I know I can do it.

I am only five years old. I know I can compete in the big sled dog race from Anchorage to Nome at least three more times, maybe five. However, I have to prove to Mr. Raymie that I will not let him down on that long trail because the pain becomes too bad and forces me to quit.

Mike set up a fundraiser to help pay for my operation. One lady in Indiana replied that she would love to help me, but she was not working and just underwent emergency surgery. However, this wonderful person wrote me that she might be able to donate. I answered her saying that I could not accept her money. She needed it more than I did. Since my buddy Mike works as an employment consultant, he gave me several contacts and web sites that I sent to that wonderful woman to help her find a job.

Mike told me a nonprofit organization called IMOM, would help with the fundraiser to pay for my operation. He said that two people, one named Linda, and one named Kerry, pushed real hard to get help for me. I sure wish I could thank everyone who has helped me. Very soon, I will have my operation, and things will be so much better for me. I owe that all to the IMOM volunteers, Dr. Jim, and so many people and fur buddies who have wished me well.

What a Great Day

Mike does not live near me, He visits Lakota and me on weekends. The last time he visited, I think I surprised him a little. Mike was giving me plenty of attention and one of the other dogs, Teacher, started to bark. Yep, a pure case of canine jealousy. My back was to Teacher and so was Mike's. As soon as Teacher started to bark, I jumped up and made a very quick 180-degree turn. I started to bark back in Teacher's direction. Teacher was saying, "Hey guy, what about me?" I told him, "Back off Teacher. Mike will get to you when he is done with me." I heard Teacher lay down, waiting for Mike to give him some attention. After Mike was done with me, he walked over to Teacher and made a big fuss over him. Mike told Teacher that he was big, strong, smart and a very good dog. I could not see Teacher's face, but I bet he was smiling and very happy about what Mike told him. I am glad, Teacher is a good friend of mine. When he was finished with Teacher, he gave all the dogs some tender loving care and made a special fuss over Lakota. Lakota and I talked. He told me that he really feels good when Mike works with him. Sounds like Lakota is starting to get over his shyness.

Mike called my name, walked over to me, and took me for a walk. Mike is teaching me voice commands so when we walk, he can tell me if stuff is in my way. It is like learning a different language. Can you picture an Alaskan Husky learning New York-eze!

During one of our walks, Mike told me that he was going to talk with Dr. Jim and set up my operation very soon. He said I would stay at his home in the city and he would take time off from work to take care of me after the operation. Mike said that once he gets all of the facts about the operation, he will tell me. He put his face right in front of mine and whispered "Pretty soon, buddy, all of that pain you feel will be gone, and I know your life will be so much better without it."

I don't know what to say. I never had anyone give me this much attention. When our walk was over, we went back to where my buddies were. There were a lot of people visiting us today and Mike would stand by my side to make sure that people did not get to close to me and startle me. I like people, but they don't realize that I can't see them. I would hate to jump around and hurt someone.

After a while, it was time to go home. I would go back to Mr. Raymie's' place and Mike would head to his home in the city. Mike told me he would see me soon. I sure hope so. I am getting to like this guy a lot. My buddies talk about him also. They really appreciate him giving them fresh water, especially since it has been so warm lately.

Doc told me that one day when it was very hot and he was not feeling well, Mike put his hands into the cold water and rubbed it all over Doc's face to cool him down. Doc said that it felt so good when Mike did that. Several of my other buddies said he did the same to them. Nitro, who is the biggest dog in the group, said that he has been around a lot of humans and he knows that Mike is a good one. When Teacher told the group what Mike had told him, and how good it made Teacher feel, the other dogs said that Mike always says good stuff to them also. They feel so happy when he does that. All the dogs said it makes them feel great. It seems that my friend Mike has made friends with all of my buddies.

Biscuits for Everyone

When Mike came to see me today, he was very excited. I heard him talking to Mr. Raymie, but I could not make out what they were saying. I was a little too far away. Soon, I heard my buddies getting very keyed up. Why, I thought? Then I heard Mike open his biscuit bag and they knew he was getting ready to give them biscuits. Mike always makes Lakota and me wait until last, but then we get two biscuits each. Mike breaks my biscuits into small pieces and puts them in his hand, under my mouth. With one finger, he tickles my chin. That is my signal that the biscuit is in Mike's open hand. I just "look" down and there it is. Lakota tells me that when Mike does this, I get all of the crumbs that I would normally drop on the ground and can not find because I can not see them.

Mike gave me a bunch of ear rubs and once I finished the biscuits, he snapped the leash on my collar, and away we went for a walk. I love to walk, all kinds of new smells and sounds to explore. Lakota asks me so many questions when I return from these walks. Maybe Mike will take both of us for walks soon.

As we were walking, Mike told me that he had some great news to tell me. He stopped walking and knelt down next to me. Mike told me that he received a letter in the mail with four checks totaling $55 donated to my surgery. He asked me if I remember the unemployed lady in Indiana. Of course I do. Mike said she raised funds for my operation!

Oh my, that is just great! Perfect strangers coming together to help a blind dog that they never met!

Mike told me that we are getting closer and closer to getting the operation done. Another week or so and we should have all of the money we need.

Well, this is going to be some adventure. Mike will pick me up after he finishes work on Tuesday. I get to ride in a big dog box on Mike's truck, get to roam in his fenced in back yard, and smell grass and all the different flowers in his garden. You know when we dogs run, we run on dirt or snowy trails and seldom get a chance to stop and smell the flowers!

Mike told me he will pitch his tent in the back yard and stay with me, since I have never been to his home before, and this is probably the first time I have ever been alone. Hope he doesn't mind if I snore!

He told me I can not eat after midnight and we must be at the eye vet's place at 8. After some paperwork, the eye vet will give me some medicine to make me go to sleep. While I am dreaming of running down the trails, he will do the surgery. They told Mike that he could come back and get me at 4:30 p.m. I will have to wear a silly looking cone thing around my head. Hope the guys back home won't see me looking that silly.

I hear I will be on medicine and eye drops for 10 days or so.

I found out that Mike has been holding out on me. He never told me his wife Mary was a great cook, or he had a lot of salmon in his freezer. Hey Mike, we need to talk, I can put away some salmon!

After Mike and I went for our walk, we sat down and Mike started to read my email to me. One email he received was from someone who wrote "that she was so happy Mike has you Rivers — or does Rivers have Mike."

Now that was an interesting statement. I had to think about that. I guess we have each other. I was lucky when Mike saw me and decided to help. He never says why he did what he did with the fundraiser and taking care of me. Maybe he does not know. I am not his dog, but he has said that I can live with him.

Humans, they are unpredictable!

Mike was telling me that he received a check, a donation, from his three cousins who live on the East Coast. Then he told me about a very nice man named Frank, who met me a few weeks ago. Frank came from New York, where Mike was born. I remember Frank, he talked with the same funny accent that Mike talks with. Sure not Alaskan!

Anyway, Mike told me that Frank and his wife, Delores, donated the rest of the money I needed for my operation.

For once in my life, I was glad that my eyes were teary. I did not want my buddies to see me cry. All of this kindness coming my way lately is totally overwhelming. How do I thank so many people who have done so much for me? What can I say? Knowing that all of these people are pitching in to help me, a blind dog, just leaves me barkless.

When I got home that night, I told all of my buddies the good news. They told me that they were very happy for me. Some of my buddies passed around treats that they had stashed away. Doc told me "See, Rivers, good things happen to those who least expect it." Then Lakota spoke up, saying, "Everything happens for the best, Rivers. However, we may never learn what the best really is." Now that is amazing, Lakota speaking up. He never does that! Leave it to Lakota to find some good in everything.

Today is the Day

I just wanted to let you know that Mike will take me to the eye vet this morning. I wanted to update my diary before the operation. I am a little scared. Nevertheless, I know that Dr. Jim and Mike are there for me. Dr. Jim told Mike that I will be ready to leave Dr. Jim's place by around 5 p.m.

Before we left for the city, Lakota told me he would miss me and he would be howling for me to have a good operation. Doc and Nitro wished me well and so did many of my other buddies. I knew I would be okay with Lakota, Doc, Nitro and the rest of the gang pulling for me.

This morning, Mike told me it was 8:45 p.m. when we arrived at his place last night. Since I can't tell time, I have no idea what he meant by that. Hmm, so this is the city!

I understand that Mike and Mary have another dog. Her name is Sandy. They put her in the house while Mike took me all around the yard on a leash. After about 10 minutes, Mike took me off the leash and let me wander all over the fenced-in the yard. Boy, I sniffed everything, fence, deck, flowers. You name it. It was all new to me. So many new scents! I heard Mike and Mary laughing. Mike said to Mary, "Look at the big smile on Rivers' face." He kept laughing as he said, "I've never seen his tail raised up so high. It must be wagging a mile a minute." She said "Rivers is really enjoying himself, isn't he." You bet I am. But what is this smile stuff? I don't ever remember smiling. Well, at least no one ever told me I smiled.

What a dinner they gave me! Mike told me that tomorrow,

after I get home from the operation, salmon is on the menu! This must be some kind of resort.

Well, I paced out the back yard and got an idea where most things were. That helps me from knocking my nose into things. Mike helps by telling me if I am getting too near something. However, we have to work on his New York City accent. Kind of hard for an Alaskan dog to understand!

Mike keeps me on a 15-foot leader when he is not in the yard with me. When he is in the yard, and the gate is closed, he lets me run free. I did find Mary's vegetable garden. Hmm, I've got to think about eating veggies. I heard Mike say that Sandy actually digs the carrots out of the ground and then eats them! Maybe she will teach me to do that.

Now I can tell that Mary is the smaller one. Got to win her over since I hear she is the better cook. But, I don't want to upset her dog, Sandy, since I am only a guest here for a week or so.

I was so excited that I had a hard time getting to sleep. I was doing real fine until that next door neighbor came home at 2 a.m. racing his motorcycle engine. Must be the city life! This morning Mike got me up and let me run in the yard a bit. Then he sat down with me, told me everything will be okay. After that he packed up my travel kennel and took me to the vet.

Recovery

Well the last few days have been a real blur. I remember Mike taking me to Dr. Jim's office. I remember falling asleep. When I woke up I had this cone thing on my head, and my eyes itched. Hey, I can live with the itch because all of that pain I had been feeling for so long is gone!

Then I realized that I was very hungry. You can bet your last dog biscuit that I was sure glad to hear Mike's voice. He put me in the big dog box on the back of his truck and took me home.

After the short ride to Mike's home, he helped me out of the big box on the back of his truck, and guided me to the back yard. Mary had this great chow ready for me. Dog food and cooked salmon! Did it smell great! They also put a hot dog in it with my pills stuffed in it. Smart idea, but I would have taken them right out of Mike's hand. Boy, that chow was super. Mary sure is a great cook.

I was very frisky, and kept bouncing into things. So that is what this cone thing is for on my head. Protect my eyes from getting hurt. It sure distorts my hearing and sense of direction. I can't get my bearings. It is very uncomfortable.

All of a sudden I became very tired and laid down. The slight pain and itch were gone. Must be the pills which I think are making me mellow. Think I went to sleep.

Mike told me that he would sleep in the backyard with me to make sure I was okay. Every once in a while I would move around a little bit to get comfortable and I could hear him talk to me, making sure I was okay, and telling me I would be alright.

I think I slept all night. I don't remember getting up at all during the night. I guess the pills wore off, and nature called, so I got Mike up. "Hey Mike, I am hungry again!" Mike went into the house to see what Mary had made for breakfast. I heard the door open and Mike walked over to me and put the food dish in front of me. I started to sniff. "Hmm," I thought, "no salmon," but I sure enjoyed those hot dogs stuffed with my pills. In a bit, the slight pain and itch were gone and I got mellow again. So, I just stretched out on the grass and took a nap.

Mike took me to see Dr. Jim again yesterday afternoon. Dr. Jim said I was doing great. He gave me some eye drops plus a shot to get the swelling down. I know Mike has been having a problem getting the eye creams into my eyes. Mike cleans them out many times a day using a warm cloth. That feels so good.

In a short time, we were back home, and it was chow time. Salmon again! Yummy. This time, there was no hot dog. Mary stuffed the pills into the salmon. Nice try, but I saved them for dessert.

It rained last night and Mike reworked the dog shelter he built. Mike told me that he opened up the entire front and rigged a tarp to act like a covered porch. It kept the deck nice and dry. I understand his tent leaks a little!

Now I know why Mike has bad hearing. His snoring just does him in! Or maybe it is this darn cone distorting the sound so much. I know one thing, his snoring must scare off any wild animals. There are wild animals in the city, right?

I let Mike sleep in this morning. I was about ready to wake him when Mary beats me to the punch. Of course, they made my breakfast with the stuffed hot dogs.

It sounds like the rain is letting up and maybe Mary and Mike will take me for a walk with Sandy. I heard Mary say that my eyes are looking much better than before the operation. Oh, they feel so much better. I can close my eyes without struggling. As I said before, besides the mild pain and itch that gets less and less each day, I am feeling no pain at all.

Mike and Mary's friend Ray came over this afternoon. I remember him visiting Mr. Raymie's place. Ray has a sled dog whose name is Junior. When Ray came over to see me, I got all excited. He had Junior's scent on him. That reminded me of Lakota and all of my buddies at Mr. Raymie's place. I can't believe that I forgot all about them since I have been here. Is that wrong?

Ray took some pictures of me. I hope Mike sends some of them to all of the nice people and my fur buddies who have written to me. I am sure he will. We spent all afternoon together. They all took turns giving me ear and belly rubs! All of us ate together in the backyard too. Even Sandy joined us. I had a great time, but I do miss my buddies.

Country Visit

What a day yesterday was! No one told me that Mike and Mary were taking me out to the country to see Lakota, Doc, Ugly, Brownie, Teacher, and the rest of the crew. It was a real surprise to me.

Mr. Raymie was very glad to see me too. He was so pleased with the results of my operation. If you think he is pleased, believe me, I am just thrilled. The eye pain is all but gone, and I can actually blink my eyes with ease.

The trip out was a little scary. Mike has a truck with this big box on the back. There are a couple of soft mats to lay on, so I was not lying on the metal floor of the truck box. It is really nice and comfortable. I was really enjoying the trip until the rain started. Now, I am an outside dog and I am very used to rain, but this was very bad stuff. It just pounded down on the box and the cone thing just increased the sound. It was scary. Soon we got to where we had to go and I had a good time visiting my buddies.

After we got back to Mike and Mary's home, Mike cleaned my eyes. He told me that they were looking very good. The swelling is almost gone, but Mike still has a problem getting the cream in my eyes. I guess that is partly my fault, since I jerk around a lot while he is trying to get my eyes open to get the cream into them.

Sandy, the family dog, does not seem to like me. Mike brought her over to me and she just growled. Maybe the cone thing scares her. She also growled at Mike. Boy, she must be very angry with him for not taking her to the country with us today. But, as soon as Mike put his coffee cup down,

Sandy started begging to slurp up the stuff. Wow, what these city dogs eat and drink!

Mike has to go back to work this week, so it will be just Sandy and me in the back yard. We are both on leaders and separate. Maybe I can talk to her and get her to be friendly to me. I guess she is an "only dog" in this family and all of the attention Mary and Mike give her just spoiled her. Boy, she sure is lucky to get all of that attention. I can understand that. Remember when Teacher got upset because Mike was giving me so much attention few weeks back?

Mike went back into the house and for some reason, I started to howl. No, it was not a pain type of howl. I guess a lonely type of howl. I am used to being alone, but maybe today being with Lakota and my other buddies, just made me a little lonely for them. I don't know, but I felt better when I was done. I wondered if my buddies heard me. I heard Mary say to Mike that it was a very beautiful howl. She really enjoyed it. I heard Mike say it was very nice as long as I was not in any kind of pain.

Mike came out and let me off the leader, so I could roam around the yard a little. I wandered into his tent. Not bad, I thought. There was this big springy dog bed in it. When I stepped on it, I started to bounce! Not for me! Mike started to laugh and lead me back to my own big soft pillow. We sat down, talked and he rubbed my tummy and top of my head, very gently, being careful not to touch my eyes. He told me I was a good dog and doing great.

Mike said he had done some research and found out that I have a sister and she lives in Northern Alaska. There are only the two of us. Our mother died a day after we were born. Some kind people raised us and that is where the research ends. Funny, I don't miss my sister, probably because I really don't know or remember her. I guess it is like being blind. You know, I have been blind for so long that I don't remember being able to see. Nah, too many heavy thoughts for a simple country dog.

Well, I guess I just dozed off, and Mike crawled back in his tent.

City Life

Well, yesterday started to be a very quiet kind of day, but it sure got exciting in the afternoon! Mike took his tent down and told me that he had to go back to work on Monday, and I would have to stay in the yard by myself. That's cool, I thought. Later in the day, Mike and Mary's granddaughter, Caitlyn, came over, and we all went for a walk. It can be very scary for a country dog to wake up in the city . There are a lot of different noises and nasty dogs barking. The trails we walked on were very hard. I think Mike called it asphalt.

We must have walked toward a creek because I heard water running over some rocks. I also found some big animal scents. Moose? Bear? Do city moose and bear smell different from country moose and bear? Moose and bears don't like dogs. They think we are wolves, who fight with them. I was getting a little tired, and we all went back to Mike's home.

Sandy did not go with us since she walks too fast and pulls too hard for walking with the baby. Mike took her out for a short walk. When Mike returned, he told Mary that Sandy had to go to the emergency vet because two dogs attacked her on the street in a residential neighborhood! She is a tough old lady, did not even cry! Mike came back from the vet and said that Sandy got three stitches in her neck.

Sandy still won't come near me, but I like hearing her in the back yard. She will come around.

Bedtime came and they took Sandy in the house to keep an eye on her neck wound. I was okay until I got up and did not bounce into the tent. I forgot! Mike is not out here with me. Oh, I was lonely, and I started to howl. Mike came out with a mat and his sleeping bag and told me it was okay. He said it was early morning. Mike stretched out on the deck with me. He is too big to get into my shelter. I laid down next to him and he rubbed my tummy, but I could not get comfortable with that cone thing on. I was restless. I actually walked over Mike several times to get to the grass and tangled him up in my leader. Mike would just pick me up, put me back in the shelter, and get me to lie down on my pillow. I would get up again.

After a while, Mike told me he was going back into the house. Mike told me that he would be right inside, and Mary could hear me if I had a problem. I did not know that. When I realized he was still very close to me and I would be okay, I went back to sleep. I guess I just missed his snoring!

When Mike came out this morning to clean out my eyes, give me breakfast and my pills, he was not angry. He said he understood that it is easy to get scared or lonely when you are alone in a strange place, and you don't know where your buddies are. He said he would pitch the tent tonight and stay outside with me.

Mike also told me that Dr Jim said I had to keep the cone on for seven to 10 days. I hope Mike will take it off soon, I really hate it.

Alone with Sandy

This was a very lazy day for me. Sandy and I were in the back yard since Mike and Mary both had to work. Mike came home at lunch time to give me my eye creams I really hate that stuff and instinctively keep my eyes closed, so Mike has a tough time getting the creams in. He also has to put the same stuff into one of Sandy's eyes and give her some pills, due to the dog bite.

Mike takes a warm face cloth and cleans the gunk from the corners of my eyes. He says the crud is getting less and less each day. It feels so good when he rubs my face with that warm cloth. Sometimes he uses a cool cloth and I rub my face up against it. Mike says that I am opening my eyes more each day, and my eyes look very good. The swelling is gone and it does not hurt to open or close my eyes anymore

I am not big on human food, but I love salmon and meat. The first things I eat are the chunks of hot dog with my pills stuffed into them. I don't even taste the pills. Boy, I am sure learning to like hot dogs! Mike and Mary ran out of the dog food they brought for me, and gave me some of Sandy's "for seniors and overweight dog food." Ugh! Very bad tasting stuff. That must be the reason why Sandy eats her dog biscuits and food so fast, and digs the carrots out of the garden.

I think Sandy got bored because she started talking to me. She told me all about herself. Sandy said that Mike and Mary rescued her about four years ago. She never had puppies. Sandy said that her last home was a very cold garage. She hardly ever went out. She had little food and never got to go for walks. Before that, Sandy said she lived with some people who like to walk a lot and treated her very well. She doesn't remember what happen to them, but she said that they were hikers, and Sandy use to hike with him. That is why she walks so fast and pulls so hard. Sandy loves to walk. When Mike and Mary got her, she was a lot heavier. Sandy said that Mary feeds her, while Mike walks and plays with her. Sandy and Mike used to go for some very long walks, but since Mike's knee has been acting up, they only go for short ones. She also told me she likes to "play catch the ball."

I asked Sandy what that was. "You mean you don't know what catch the ball is?" She asked. "No." I replied, "What is it?"

"It is a game that dogs play with their human companions," she said. "Some humans use a tennis ball others use a stick. They throw it and we catch or fetch it."

I guess I looked confused because Sandy said "How about the tugging game. Have you ever played that?"

"No, I never played any games." I told her.

"Mike plays both of those games with me." she said. She told me all about these games.

"Do you think Mike would play the games with me?" I asked. "Catch the ball may be tough since you can't see." she said. "But some balls have noise makers in them, so you probably could find them when they made noise. The tugging game should be no problem. Just remember that Mike will not play the tugging game with food. If he gives you a biscuit or a bone, he will not try to take it away from you or tug on it while you are eating it." Then she added, "He may try to play the tugging game with you with a fat piece of rope or a rubber stick, or a tugging toy. Maybe, after your eyes are healed up, he will teach you."

We talked all afternoon, and she told me about many things I did not know. She talked about rawhide bones, cow hooves and other things she gets to chew. From what she was telling me; I must live a sheltered life in the country.

When Mike came home, he put the tent up very fast. I heard him and Mary talking about how bad the clouds looked and I thought I heard thunder. Yes, it did rain, but I was dry and comfortable. After a while, Mike came back out and sat with me, rubbed my tummy. He told me he couldn't wait to get this cone thing off me, so he can rub my neck. Yeah, I can't wait either.

Some very wonderful fur buddies and people have written to me about being outside, and not in Mary and Mike's house. I really appreciate their concern, but I don't remember ever been inside. I would not know how to act. Besides, that is Sandy's home and she tends to get very jealous.

Mike did talk to Mary about me moving into the house for a while. I heard them say that the house is too small with too many things I could bounce into and get hurt. One more thing is that I may not be housebroken. I think that means that I would go to the bathroom in the house and not outside. Wouldn't that wear out my welcome real fast?

Mike tried to get me to stay in the tent with him, but I'd rather stay outside. Besides, I have a big soft pillow for a bed and I stay in a very dry area. I am very happy and get a lot of attention. Anyway, Mike sleeps in his tent outside with me, so I am not alone. During the daytime, Sandy is outside with me and Mike comes home from work for lunch to take care of my eyes.

I like being outside and since I am an Alaska Husky, I love the cold temperatures. Mike told me this morning, before he left for work, that there is fresh snow in the mountains! I can't wait.

I heard a flock of geese fly overhead today. They are in training for their flight south. That means winter, my season, and snow. Did I tell you I like snow?

The Rainbow Bridge

Yesterday was a nice day. I can open my eyes more. Mike took the cone off me for a bit last night and took me for a walk. Wow! It felt good to get that thing off. The walk was fine, but Mike lives in a very busy neighborhood. I heard many dogs barking and once in a while Mike would yell, "back, back." I thought Mike was yelling at me, but he told me that he was yelling at the stray dogs or the ones whose owners let them run loose. They seem to listen to him, since they did not come near us.

There are many nasty kids living where Mike lives. He has to walk around them, since they block the street. Not old teenagers, young kids. I don't like them.

While we were walking on a very hard trail, I heard this rushing, whooshing sound come from behind us. I jumped and got real scared. Mike told me it was a big truck and there was nothing fear. He said the truck was not near us. The trail the truck was on must be right next to the trail we were walking. That truck sounded so close to us.

When we got home, Mike put the cone back on me, and got some of the email that many people write to me. He reads them to me. I like being near people. When they talk, especially if they talk to me, I feel I am part of their group. That is so nice, especially since I have been alone for so long.

One of my fur buddies suggested this trick. Since Mike has a beard, maybe he should use peanut butter for grooming it. Mike, being a smart human companion, caught on that it was a way for me to get a sweet treat. "Nice try," he said as he went back into the house.

Rivers

A short time later, Mike came out, gave me my nightly tummy rub. He then crawled into his tent. He leaves the front flap open so that he can keep an eye on me. Soon, I heard him snoring and I fell asleep myself.

However, before I did, I howled a little, very softly so that I would not wake Mike. Humans don't realize that some dogs howl because that is how we pray. I have a lot to be thankful for. Mike told me that several of the fur buddies, who email me, need our prayers because they are very sick. Others have crossed over the "Rainbow Bridge."

Mike explained to me what the "Bridge" was. He told me that our real fears, pain and hurt are only in this world. He also said that a person, greater than any human in this world, put us here for a reason, but we may never know that reason. It could be to bring joy and happiness or sadness to our human companions, who love us so very much. Mike told me that the "Bridge" is very beautiful place, where there is no pain or sick dogs. We will be totally well. Mike told me I would be able to see when I go there. I would also meet some of his dogs, his fur buddies, he sent there, when they got too sick to have a good life with Mike.

Does that mean that I would see Mike there? How would I know him? I don't know what he looks like. Mike said it is also a special place in the hearts of our humans companions where no harm or hurt or illness will ever come to us. It will be our time to rest when our job here, in this world, is done,

I was thinking about what Mike had said when he told me about one of the people who emails me. This person asked us to pray for one of her family members, a baby, who was very ill. The baby was born too early and was having a very hard time hanging on to her life. I guess that is why I howled, my way of praying for that little baby, my sick fur buddies, and being so thankful for all the good things that have happen to me.

It was a very peaceful night.

The Cone Comes Off Today!

It was rather cool for Mike last night, but great sleeping weather for me. I am getting use to Mike's loud snoring. Besides letting me know he is there, it keeps the wild city animals away. I was wondering if his neighbors would complain about his loud snoring. I guess I had that look on my face when I have a question, because I heard Mike started to laugh. "My snoring bothering you, Rivers?" he said. "Or are you worried that my neighbors may complain?" My ears perked up, telling Mike I understood what he was saying. He just started to laugh some more and said "Rivers, who is going to call the cops on an old geezer like me and complain about my snoring?" He was right. I had nothing to worry about, so I stretched out on my pillow.

Later that night, I woke up and heard Mike leaving the tent to go into the house for a few minutes. When he returned, I heard him standing a few feet from my shelter. I raised my head (that darn cone makes a lot of noise) and Mike said, as if he knew my question, that he was just looking at the stars and the moon. He told me that the sky was very clear and it was unusual for him to see the stars, due to the city lights. He sat with me a few moments, describing to me what he saw, while rubbing the top of my head and behind my ears. I fell asleep and did not notice that he went back into the tent.

Have you ever wondered how dogs tell time? We do not. Those that can see have an idea of what part of the day it is if is light or dark. Blind dogs can not do that, so we rely on what happens around us. For example, I know that when Mary calls Mike to get up, and she lets Sandy out, it is time for me to get up also. Chow will be coming soon. I guess that is what you call routine. So, when Mike comes out to say good-bye, it is time for him to work. I know it will be a while before he will come back home. So I crawl back on my bed or lay in the strawberry patch and snooze.

Well, when Mike came home last night, he told me the cone was coming off. Yippee! I was so excited that I forgot I was on a leader, took off full speed, and bounced into the picnic table. Caught it in the chest, just as I heard Mike yell "watch out" and the leader pulled me back. No damage done, except to my pride, which went away as soon as Mike caught up to me and started to rub my chest. Wow! It is a whole new world without that cone thing on me. Smells and sounds are different.

Some friends of the family came over. Frank was here right after my operation, but I don't remember him. Mike says he is a real nice guy, had has two dogs of his own, but I just could not go near him. I just cruised back to the strawberry patch and enjoyed the night air and listened to their voices.

Pretty soon Mary came out, and said Sandy was scratching the stitches she got from the dog attack. Mike put the cone thing on her so she could not get to her wound. I heard her bounce that cone thing into a lot of stuff. She is a big dog and that cone sticks out wider than she does. So she tends to misjudge the space she needs to move in. She will be okay.

Mike read me an email I received from a fur buddy's human companion. They were concerned about the yard I am staying in. Well, Mike told me that there is a big wooden fence all around the yard and it has a locked gate. There are houses on three sides. It is a small yard with raised garden and flowerbeds on one side. Sandy stays over there guarding her veggies. The back fence is lined with raspberry bushes, with thorns that pricked my nose. My shelter is under the dining room window on a large deck. On one side of the deck is a tall wooden shed and on the other side is the fence. Mike's tent is about 10 feet in front of me. It is very nice and cozy.

Well, it is time for Mike to clean out my eyes. He says that the left eye looks almost normal and the right eye is progressing just as the Dr. Jim said it would. I wonder what color they were. He says I look like a very normal dog with nice brown eyes. "A very handsome dog," Mike added.

I wonder what I do look like.

Moose, Trails and Guard Duty

Today was not a bad day. I feel real good and my eyes do not crud up as much as they used to. It feels good to open them.

I can tell it is cloudy today, because it was not too cool last night. Feels like it might rain.

Sandy is in the yard with me and I know she is not a happy camper. She still has the cone thing on. I hope it will come off her soon. I know how uncomfortable it is to wear that thing. "Hang in there, Sandy. Mike will take it off you soon." I told her. She said "I sure hope so. This thing is the pits to wear." Her stitches are bothering her, I bet they itch a little, but that will pass. Yep, kind of a lazy day for both of us.

Mike came home for lunch and cleaned the crud from my eyes. He gave Sandy her pills and eye medicine. When it was my turn for the eye medicine, I started to fuss like normal, but he held me very tight and got a good dose into each eye. It feels so good when he is done. I do not know why I give him such a battle with it. I sure like it when he rubs that soft wet cloth over my face.

He sat down with us and ate his lunch. He offered some to Sandy and she just gobbled it down. Me, I did not like it. I think he said it was a chunk of cheddar cheese. He offered me a cracker and I would not eat that either. He tossed it to Sandy. I guess she caught it. All I heard was her teeth chomping on it. She doesn't miss too many treats that are tossed her way.

I decided to take an afternoon nap and then the rain started. I moved from the strawberry patch to my shelter and listened to the rain come down. Wow, it sure rained hard. Mary came home and took Sandy inside. Mike came home a little after Mary. I heard his truck pull up in the driveway. In a short while, I heard them come out of the house with my chow. I sniffed the bowl. This was good stuff! Mixed in with my dog food and the hot dogs with the pills in them, was some kind of meat. I think Mary called it country fried steak. Was that good! Licked my bowl super clean. Yep, a full belly and another nap is in order.

The rain stopped and Mike took me for a walk. There was a light mist still coming down. It was so cool and clean smelling. It was very quiet and still. We walked over to the woods where the trail is by the creek. I just had a field day sniffing and smelling everything. Mike saw a rainbow and was telling me all about it. Yes, I could see it in my mind, but to be honest, I was more interested in the smells. I thought I smelled salmon and Mike told me that the creek has a run of salmon each year. Down where he lives, he does not get bears, but up the creek, about five miles, they do.

How did I miss the moose? It must have been the excitement of the trail. I am sure glad Mike saw it blocking our way. Mike said it was about 50 feet up the trail. Once he stopped walking, I caught wind of the moose. I have never been this close to a moose before. Mike told me that the moose was looking at us and for me to be very still. I turned around to face the way we came, with my back to the moose. I am trained to run from moose. Sled dogs are no match for a 1000 pounds of angry moose. Mike was telling me that the moose just stared at us. He said that once the moose realized we were not a threat, it started to nibble on some tree branches.

Soon we started to walk back home. I heard some other dogs barking and Mike just called out to them. He told them that they were good puppies, and they stopped barking. Pretty big dogs from the sound of their bark. Once we got home, Mike left me off the leader so I could wander around the yard a little. I thought I heard something from around the strawberry patch. I walked over to it and Mike hitched me up to my leader since Mary said Sandy had to go out.

Now what is that sound?

A short while later, Mike came back out to clean my eyes and get ready to go to bed in the tent. I was by the strawberry patch smelling and listening. Mike started to laugh and told me it was either the neighbor's dog or a shrew that he had seen by the fence a few weeks ago. He sat by my shelter and called me, but I was too interested in that sound and smell. "You are going to miss your belly rubs," he said, but I just ignored him and patrolled the fence and strawberry patch. I heard the zipper to the tent zip open and then zip close. In no time at all, the snoring started. Okay, I got the hint. It was bedtime. It was getting cooler and the wind picked up. I curled up on my dry soft pillow, in my shelter, and closed my eyes. I was just drifting off when I heard Mike say. "Good boy, Rivers. Get some sleep."

The Weekend

What a busy, and at times rainy, lazy weekend. Friday was a nice, clear day and cool. You could tell that winter is on its way to Alaska. Sandy and I loafed in the yard, gabbing about our human companions. While we do talk, she won't come near me, but checks my shelter to see if I have any goodies stashed away. Mike will put a dog biscuit in my shelter for me to nibble on during the night. Sandy and I are very different. I like to eat very slow and will stop when I am full. She gobbles her food down and probably won't stop until she explodes!

Since it was so clear Friday, the night got cold. Mike forgot that I am an outdoor dog and enjoy this kind of weather. He pulled a blanket out of Sandy's doghouse to put over me. I was half-asleep, since the tummy rubs Mike gave me made me sleepy. I did not notice what he was doing. I was starting to dose off. When he put the blanket over me, I thought Sandy was trying to lie on top of me! She is 90 pounds and I am only 50. I got scared and jumped up and knocked Mike down! I had no idea what was happening until I heard Mike laughing as he said, "It is only me, Rivers." When he put the blanket on me, he started to wrap it around me and I felt him hug me. I actually thought it was Sandy trying to get into my shelter! Mike said it took 20 minutes to settle me down to the point where I would go back into the shelter.

After I got back in the shelter and had a second dose of belly rubs, Mike crawled into his tent and sleeping bag. It got cold, into the 30s was my guess. I know there was frost on the ground and some ice floating in my water bucket. My kind of weather, but I guess not Mike's. I really heard his bones creaking that morning when he crawled out of the tent. He went into the house. Very soon, Mike came out of the house with my breakfast. Warm dog food with bits of baloney in it. Guess I am getting a little fussy. I picked out the baloney and left most of the dog food. After that, we had one of our three times a day wrestling matches to get the medicine into my eyes.

A short while later, Mike clips on my leash and says we are going out. All right, a walk! I know I am out the gate because I can smell my favorite trash can. Just ahead is that big rock I like so well. Mike tugs on the leash for me to go to the right and I feel the asphalt on the bottom of my feet. Mike picks me up and puts me into the big box on the back of his truck. We are going for a ride! All right, where to?

The big box has two sliding windows with screens on them. Mike is heading out of the city. I can smell the different scents in the air. Wow! This is just great. I have no idea how far we went, and I do not know how long we drove. After a while, we stopped and Mike let me out of the big box on the back of his truck. Surprise! There were all of my buddies. Mike told me to go with my buddies while he did some chores with Mr. Raymie. Lakota told me he was so glad to see me and was worried about me being in the city. There was Nitro and Teacher telling me about the new girl in town. Doc, who is very gentle and smart, asking me about my operation, and how I was doing. There was Terror telling me my eyes looked very well. He said I put on some weight. Brownie and Lucky asked how Mike is treating me. Finally Ugly, who really is not ugly, asking me when I am coming home. We spend the better part of the day talking. I was telling them about the city, the moose, the stray dogs, and Mike sleeping in a tent to keep an eye on me. They really laughed at that.

Every once in a while, Mike would give us all biscuits and ear rubs. He made sure we had plenty of fresh water because all of this talking was making us thirsty. I heard Mr. Raymie tell Mike that I looked terrific. My coat was nice and shinny and my eyes looked almost normal.

I have no idea how long we stayed in the country, but Mike had to get back to the city. He told Mr. Raymie that we would be back out on Sunday to help with some chores. Mike put me back in the big box for the trip back to the city. The truck has a window separating us. I heard the window slide open and I could put my head through it and hear Mike talking. I heard someone singing *Smoke on the Water* and then I took a nap.

Sunday came and it was raining. We still went to the country and took Mary and Sandy with us. I had to ride in my travel kennel because Sandy does not go near me. Mary calls the big box on the back of Mike truck "Sandy's RV." I am not sure what they mean by that.

It was raining very hard when we got to their friend Ray's home. Remember I wrote that Ray has a sled dog named Junior, who is my friend. We talked a bit. Ray and Mike said they were going over to Mr. Raymie's place to help with the chores. They said it would be best for us dogs to stay at Ray's place where we would stay dry. We all took naps, and before we knew it, it was time to return to the city.

It was raining when we got home. Mike fed us and soon it was time for bed. A little after that, Mike came out gave me a whole bunch of tummy rubs and then crawled into his tent. It rained all night.

Walking My Last City Trail

Boy, I guess Mike just don't like Mondays. He was sure sluggish getting out of the tent this morning. Come on, Mike, I am raring to go! Yes I know it is cold and I know it is rainy, but ... What did you say? You've got to go to work! No wonder you don't like Mondays.

I was depressed, I figured Mike would be home and we could go for another walk or something. I don't even remember what I had for breakfast. What a bummer! What a minute, Mike is coming back with Mary. What is he doing? Oh that feels so good when he cleans my eyes with that warm face cloth. But Mary is with him. That means one of two things: food or medicine. It is medicine! They are gonna try putting that cream into my eyes. I will show them, I will hold them real tight. Here we go. Wait a minute. What kind of hug did Mike put on me? I cannot move. I feel the cream, and it feels so good. Now I feel the warm cloth again. Well, the show is over. Time for them to go to work.

Last night, Mike and I went for a walk. We walked down to the creek. I am getting accustomed to the sounds and scents in his neighborhood. I was having a field day with all the stuff to smell. We must have walked about a quarter of a mile and I could hear the water bubbling in a creek. I heard a couple of humans pass us. Mike said they were on bicycles. We turned around a bend, and we found a spot where I could walk into the water. I was a little leery at first, but the cool water felt good on my paws. Mike talks to me all of the time about what is around us. I can picture it all in my mind.

Instead of going back the way we came, we took the longer

route. The trail must have passed through some very tall trees, since it became very cool. We walked up a little hill and then back on to what must be a main trail, since I heard a lot of cars around us.

Mike shortened up on my leash and kept talking, to saying everything was okay. Boy, this country dog is sure getting a city education! The sun did come out during our walk, but it must have gone behind some clouds, because it sure got cool again.

It was getting close to bedtime. Soon Mike came out and started with my nightly body hugs. He would stop and then I hit him with my paw and give him my "Can I have more" look. He gave me some more, talked to me, and rubbed my ears. He stopped and I would hit him again with my paw and give him another poor pitiful me look and he started again. Nope, he did not fall for it the third time. Instead he told me "Good night" and I heard the tent zipper open and close. In a few minutes, that fog horn snoring started, and I knew he was out cold.

At least I thought so, but we both heard this whistle sound, I got up to investigate and I heard him roll over to watch me. How can anyone sleep lightly through that snoring sound he makes? I checked out the fence and did not notice anything different. However, I was wide awake and knew Mike was not going to come out of the tent to give me more belly rubs. So I figured I would just go visit him.

I poked my nose into the front of the tent and some kind of material stopped me. I heard Mike laugh and heard the zipper move. All of a sudden, I knew I could just walk right into the tent.

Hey this is pretty neat. I do not like this noisy plastic stuff on the floor, but it is dry. Wow, what a bed Mike sleeps on! I poked around and investigated all of it and then I sat down. I guess I was sitting at the head of the bed and looking down at Mike. I got up and turned around and before I knew it, he pulled me into the bed with him! My head was on one arm and his other was around my back, rubbing my belly. I was pressed right up to him and the top of my head was under his chin.

This is really comfortable! A nice soft bed, dry, and getting my belly rubbed all at the same time! What a real lucky dog I am. It is getting a little warm for me. But it sure feels good. Then it dawned on me, am I becoming a lap dog? What if Lakota or my buddies found out? Nitro and Brownie and the rest of them would tease me about being a wimp. Rivers a wimp! No way! With that thought racing through my mind, I bolted out of the tent and walked around the yard.

I heard Mike chuckling, and every once in a while I would poke my head in through the opening of the tent. What am I to do? I walked over to my shelter to lie down on my pillow. Soon I heard the zipper zipped, Mike started to snore, and I drifted off to dreams of running down the trails.

My Last Day In The City

It was sure rainy and windy last night. I was nice and dry, but I really wondered if the tent would come down. It rained very hard and the wind blew all night. I thought about going into the tent with Mike, but the way the wind was blowing, I was afraid the tent would come down on us. So I curled up in my shelter and worried about Mike sleeping in the tent. It blew all night and I bet he did not sleep too well.

I am sure enjoying my trail walks with Mike. They get longer and longer each day. There was a break in the rain and we took off. He was telling me how high the water was in the creek. We had the entire trail to ourselves, since there were no people, dogs or moose out. It seems that the rain washed away all of my trail markings. Oh well, I guess a trail marker's work is never done!

Since last night was the last night that I would be staying here, I thought I would see if I could curl up with Mike and sleep in the tent. He left the flap open and I wandered in. This really is not too bad. Dry, and the bed is nice and soft, kind of springy. I think Mike said he uses an air mattress. Well he moved over and I laid down on it. He wrapped one arm over my back and started rubbing my belly and I had my head resting on his arm. It was nice, but neither one of us was comfortable. I was falling off the edge of it and Mike could not get the sleeping bag to cover his shoulders. I could not curl into a ball and he could not get warm. We both moved around and finally I left. Oh well, maybe next time.

Today they tried some new stuff on me for breakfast, hot

dogs with scrambled eggs. The hot dogs were great, but the eggs, well, they are still in my bowl. Sandy was loose in the yard while Mike was out there, and she kept edging over to my food bowl. I kept hearing Mike say "No Sandy" and she would back off.

We were soon off to see Dr. Jim. Sandy had to go too, since she had a follow up visit for her eye problems. Mike took her in first and after she came back, I went in. I remembered this place and I was a little hesitant, but Mike was right there and he said I would be okay.

Dr. Jim examined my eyes. He is very gentle and very good, but when he wanted to remove the stitches, I started to fuss. It took Dr. Jim, his assistant and Mike to hold me so Dr. Jim could get to the stitches. He did put drops in my eyes, but I still fussed. Dr. Jim said that I was a good dog and really strong, but he had to get the stitches out. I guess I am sensitive about anyone around my eyes. They hurt me for so long. Well, Dr. Jim finally got them out and boy, do I feel better. I can open them up really wide with no pain. Sure they are a little red, but Dr. Jim said, in a month or so, they will look normal. In fact, Dr. Jim wants Mike to bring me back in a month for a follow-up and pictures. He said I could go home.

Home! Which home? Back to the country or in the city with Mike and Mary? Never thought about it too much, but I really have two homes. I did not think I could be happy and sad at the same time, but I am. I am happy that I am going back with Lakota and my buddies Nitro, Terror, Ugly, Doc, Lucky, Brownie, and Teacher. But, I am sad that I won't be with Mike every day and I will miss him taking care of me. Sure, I will see him on weekends, but.... Oh well, sure glad my eyes are still tearing a little, don't want to be accused of crying and being a wimp.

Dr. Jim told Mike that I could go back to work, but only light duty. I could do some light training to get me ready to make the team

Mike told us that he had emailed all of the humans and my fur buddies, who wrote to me, telling them I was a racing sled dog. He said he was not bragging about me. Rather, he wanted to let them know that they can do anything they want to do and overcome any challenges they face. All it takes is the desire to do so and believe in themselves. Mike reminded them that this comes from within them. Just because they may be blind or deaf or face other physical challenges don't mean their life is over. Sure, they cannot see their favorite ball or hear the sound of their human companion's voice, but they can do a lot of other things. Actually, anything they want to do as long as they have the desire to do it.

Mike also mentioned to them that with a loving human companion in their corner, my fur buddies would not fail. I was impressed when he told me he wrote that they don't have to be a champion racing dog, or a blue ribbon show dog to succeed. All they have to do is be themselves. And you know what? Doing that makes a huge impact on the life and heart of our human companions. I must remember that no matter what my challenges are, no matter what I can not do any more, it really makes no difference to the human companion who loves me.

Mike's job allows him to work with people who need help finding jobs. He has been using me as a model for some of his clients. He says "This dogs is blind, yet Rivers raced over 1000 miles to Nome two times. What is your excuse for losing your way in life?"

My goal is to make the team and race to Nome. I have not raced in nearly two years. Besides getting back into shape, I must prove to Mr. Raymie that I will not let him down on the trail. Will I do it? You betcha, but if I don't, I know I gave it my best shot, and Mike will not love me any less.

I am so thankful. I can't believe the amount of email, prayers, and love sent my way by perfect strangers. It just adds to my desire to succeed.

My First Weekend Back Home

You would not believe the number of emails I received this week. It seems my story has touched many of my fur buddies and their human companions. I am really honored. I am trying to answer each and every one of the emails I received. My paws go fast on the trail, but are limited as to how fast they can type out email.

I saw Mike twice in the last few days It was good to see him. He gave me hot dogs and left over steak he and Mary had. Boy, was that stuff good. He told me that Sandy was upset that she did not get the scraps, but they gave her a few extra biscuits. She was a happy camper after that.

While Mike was cleaning my eyes and face, he asked me if I was giving Mr. Raymie the same battle that I gave him regarding the eye medicine. Sure, I mean, let's spread the fun, right?.

After Mike cleaned my eyes, we went for a walk. The start of the trail to Nome is a mile or so from where I live. I wanted to go to that trail, but Mike did not have his walking shoes on. Well, that was what he gave me for an excuse. I think he was afraid we would end up in Nome, and I don't think he can walk as fast as I can navigate down the trails.

I was pulling Mike real hard and racing through the puddles, sniffing everything in sight and marking the trail. I heard him laugh as he kept trying to reign me in. I was having a real blast, but like all good things, it came to an end. It was time to turn around and head home.

Mike slowed me down some and I really enjoyed myself. The trail we took runs parallel to the big trail used by the big trucks that scared me. Mike told me it was okay. We got back home and Mike put me on top of my doghouse. It has a flat roof. I have never been up there before, but my buddies tell me they do it all the time. Sunbathing, they say.

Mike started to do his famous ear and tummy rub. OOOOH, that felt so good! After a bit, he put me down on the ground and brushed me out a little. I wanted to jump up on the roof again, but missed. Mike chuckled and told me to wait until the next time he came over, and he put me back up there.

I guess there is a lot about being a dog I don't know about. I am not a big licker, and there are times I have to wonder why other dogs do things like chase a ball or play tug of war with an old rope. Remember, Sandy told me about those things. I hope Mike will teach me that stuff.

Mike said he is going to build me a new doghouse, once he figures what size I need. Well I told him I would need space for the TV, HBO, and the recliner! Only kidding. All we sled dogs need is enough space to stand up and turn around, something soft and dry on the floor, and shelter from the wind. But, if you want to add a TV, HBO and a recliner, that would be okay with me! Mike said that his friend Ray is building a new house for Junior, since he will be doing his sled dog training with Mr. Raymie.

Mike had to go back to the training track, where Lakota and my buddies are training. He told me he would see me next Saturday. The training track is about 10 miles from home. Mike told me that I would be going to the training track once I got the final okay from Dr. Jim later this month. I can't wait.

A while later Lakota came back from training and told me he had seen Mike at the track. Lakota was interested in what Mike and I did together today. Lakota said Mike gave all the dogs fresh water, biscuits, and some ear rubs. As Lakota was talking to me, the rest of my buddies came over to visit with us. Some said they were jealous that Mike did not rub their bellies. Nitro, the biggest, told everyone to simmer down. He said that Rivers and Lakota need some special attention at this time and he (Nitro) is sure that we all would get belly rubs when Mike has a chance to do that. Then Nitro says "Doesn't he reach under your harness and gives you a rub every once in a while?" They all nodded yes. "So what are you beefing about?" With that, the team went to their houses and waited for chow time. Nitro waited until the team was gone and told Lakota and me that when it comes to training and running the trails, he wanted to be our running mate. He said he take care of both of us. Thanks Nitro.

Trouble With Spot

It started out frosty this morning, but after the sun came out, it warmed up. I was getting a little concerned since Mr. Raymie did not take any of my buddies to the training track this morning, and Mike has not come yet. I found out that Mr. Raymie gave my buddies a day off since it was such a nice day. I guess Mr. Raymie wanted a day off also. Where's Mike? He is very late. He did tell me he would be here.

Spot, who is a lead dog, yelled over to me that Mike is not coming. "Come on, Rivers, get a life," he said. "You think that human companion really cares about you? He did Mr. Raymie a favor and got your eyes fixed. It's over—he's gone. Why would anyone want a blind dog?"

Spot can be a mean one. His words hurt. Maybe Spot is right. Maybe Mike will not come any more. Why would Mike want me, a blind dog, anyway? I don't know how to play the games Sandy described to me. I can't walk next to Mike without being on a leash. I crawled back into my doghouse. I was very sad and hurt. I was scared that maybe Spot was right.

Then I heard Lakota say to Spot. "What is your problem? Mike will be here. You are just jealous because Rivers gets more attention than you do. Mike gives you biscuits and ear rubs too, but you could care less. Well, I like Mike. He may give Rivers more attention than he gives me, but Rivers needs more. Rivers has worked just as hard as any of us when he ran with us." Then Nitro added, "You know, Spot, you ain't such a hot shot leader if you got to be so mean. I don't think I want to run with you any more."

Then I heard Doc, the gentle one, say, "Nitro is right, Spot. You are just mean to say that stuff to Rivers. He has never asked for any special help because he is blind. Rivers has always come through for us. So why are you being so mean to him?" Ugly spoke up next, saying "Yeah Spot, I would rather have Doc and Terror as my leaders. I will run with Rivers and Lakota any time."

Then they started to say how Mike treats them all special, and if he did not get here today, there was some good reason for it. "You guys are nuts to go bonkers over a some human who you see once a week." Spot snorted. "You can't depend on humans." He then went inside his doghouse.

A little while later, Lakota said to me, "Hey Rivers, guess whose red truck just rolled up?" I jumped out of my doghouse when I heard, "Yo, Rivers buddy, how ya doing," in that unmistakable accent. I jumped up at him and he just held me up, rubbing my tummy and telling me how good it was to see me. I think he said my tail was going 50 miles an hour. Then I smelled the bag of goodies he brought for me. Hot dogs, a hamburger, and a bunch of biscuits that he broke up and stashed in my doghouse. I shared this stuff with Lakota.

His visit was too short, but we did go for a long walk on the trail. He gave me a lot of attention, and told me he was sorry for being late. Then Mike said he would be right back after he gave my buddies some biscuits.

I heard him talked to them as he gave them treats. He even gave Spot one. Spot just grumbled as he took it. I heard Mike chuckle as Spot ate the biscuit.

Mike came back up to my doghouse and told Lakota and me about his promotion and his new job. He told us Mary and Sandy were doing fine, and that he is receiving a lot of email from my friends who are pulling for me. He read me some of their email.

Soon Mr. Raymie returned and he and Mike talked about some projects that they were going to do soon. They decided that they would not run me until Dr. Jim did his final check on me, at the end of this month.

After they finished talking, Mike came back over to me and measured my old doghouse. I stood right next to him. Every so often he would grab me, rub my back or chest, and then continue measuring. When he was done, he got a face cloth, wet it, and cleaned up my face. Mike told me that the eye gunk is almost gone and I am not tearing as much as before the operation. He told me my eyes are looking better every day.

I wondered if he knew what Spot had said to me because Mike said, "I think about you every day, Rivers. It bothers me that I can not keep you at my place in the city. We both have to hang tough and take the most we can out of these visits. I know you got good friends here with Lakota, Nitro, Doc, Terror, Brownie, and Ugly and the rest of the team. You got a job to do and that is to make the team. I may not be able to see you but once a week, but remember my thoughts are with you every day." Mike said, "You will do good."

Then Mike told me he had to go, gave me a very long hug, told me he would see me next Saturday. Then he left.

I hate it when he goes, but I know he has to. I was going back into my doghouse as Doc, Ugly, Terror, Teacher, Brownie and Nitro came by. Doc said, "You okay, Rivers?"

Before I could answer, Ugly said, "Spot can be really mean but don't listen to him."

"Yeah" Lakota said, "Didn't I tell you Mike would come to visit you. He is pretty cool for a human. I like him. He treats us all like, well, like his buddies."

We talked for a few minutes about what had happened and then I went back to my doghouse. While I felt sad that Mike had to go, I was very happy that I had so many good friends. I found one of the biscuits that Mike hid in the doghouse and thought how lucky I was.

Ray's Yard

Yo sleeping dog, you gonna get up today?" What the…. Ouch, that hurt. I hit my head on the roof of my doghouse when I jumped up. What a dream! I thought I heard Mike's voice. "Come on sleepy head. It is time to go, we don't have all day!"

It is Mike! What is he doing here so early? "Hi Rivers, how you doing?" as he rubs my head and just puts this big hug on me.

My tail is waging a mile a minute and I am trying to jump up, but he just holds me and keeps rubbing my belly. Next I heard the click of the leash and we are off.

He is telling me we are going to spend the day at his friend Ray's house. Mary, Sandy, and Junior are there. He and Ray are working on building something so he came to get me to spend the day with all of them.

The next thing I know, Mike is picking me up and putting me in the travel kennel.

Mike gives me a few biscuits and tells me he will be right back. He wants to give some biscuits to Lakota, Nitro, Doc, Ugly, Brownie, Teacher, and the rest of the team. He chuckles, and says "Even Spot." I can hear them all and they are just so happy to see him. When he gets back to the truck, he tells me he has to get my water and food bowls, since Mary has cooked up something special for me. My mouth is watering already!

We head out. Mike starts to talk to me about what has gone on this last week. He tells me about the snow in the mountains and the color of the leaves, which are turning yellow and gold. He even starts singing some song about me running and marking the trails. I really can't take it, I really can't. The words are okay, but that voice! I tried to shut out that horrid sound with my paws up against my ears. Oh please have mercy. Put the radio on!

Now don't get me wrong, I am one grateful puppy for all that Mike has done for me, but the dude can not sing and that New York City accent is hard to take when he sings cowboy music. Luckily, it is a short drive to Ray's house.

What a welcome I got! Mike clips on the leash and leads me over to a tree where my long leader is. Mary comes over and pats my head. What! No chow yet! Hey, I am a growing puppy. She must have read my mind because she slips me a hot dog. Hmm, very tasty.

Sandy is a little behind me, but we can't touch. She is very friendly and asks me how I am doing. She is a little frustrated because I can not tell her how her neck wound looks. As if Mike read her mind, he walks over to both of us. While he is patting us both on the head, he tells Sandy that her neck wound has completely healed. The fur is growing back very quickly.

Well what about me? How do my eyes look? Mike continued to pet the both us and asked Sandy, "Don't you think Rivers' eyes look a lot better, Sandy? Why they are looking better each day." Sandy told me that they looked very good. Still a little red and cloudy, but a lot better than last week. She reminded me that we both go to see the eye vet in two weeks.

"Hey, Rivers, how you doing? Welcome to my yard, partner." It was Junior. He is really a nice guy. His father is Spot. This year, Junior will start training to be a lead dog on the team. I bet he will be a great one. We talked a lot about sled dog racing. Since I have run several of them. Junior was all ears.

Speaking of ears, Ray started rubbing my ears, and just giving me all kinds of attention. This was real nice. Then Mike came over and told me that they were going to make a lot of noise for most of the day. They were building something for Ray's house, and they did not want me to get scared if I heard stuff I did not know. They told me I was no more than 10 feet away from them.

I sniffed around a little and…. Hey wait a minute, what is this? Why, it is my bed, the one I used at Mike's place. Let me check this out. Yep, just as comfortable as it was on the windy and cool nights at Mike's house.

I heard Mike and Ray talking, plus some noises that I did not recognize. I just rested on my bed, or sniffed around, or talked to Junior and Sandy. She is a very different lady dog when she is not in her own back yard, Very friendly. Occasionally, Mike, Ray, or Mary would come over to where I was, rub my ears, and give me a biscuit or a tummy rub. Sandy and Junior also got a lot of attention.

Sometimes Mike would come over to my bed, if I was on it, and just lay down beside me and we would start to wrestle. I never did this before, but I catch on quickly. This is great! He would rub me and grab me, then shake me up a little. I would break free and start to run, but stop because I can't see. I know I wanted to run around and then charge him, but....

That doesn't stop me. I would stop suddenly, then change direction, jump up on my back legs, and put my front paws on whatever part of Mike I would land on. He would laugh and we would play some more. Then he would go and play like that with Sandy.

This went on for most of the day. I did not know how much work they had to do, but I did know that it must be getting close to suppertime. Mary is frying chicken on the porch. Now, I am not a big chicken eater, but this stuff smelt very good.

I heard Ray ask Mary what she was cooking for us dogs. She told me hot dogs, beef scraps, leftovers. What! No dog food! Must be a holiday!

Chow came a little while later. I had a hard time finding the food dish filled with all of this great food. Too many great smells. So Mike put the bowl in front of my nose and put a hot dog my mouth. No problem now, as I put my head into the bowl and eat a super good meal.

Well it is getting cooler; the sun must be leaving the sky. I hear Ray and Mike come out of the house. There are two dogs in the yard next to us. Nice friendly guys. However, one of them was barking up a storm. Next, I heard Sandy and Junior barking. So, I started to bark too. It was a long time since I barked. I forgot what I sounded like. Whoa, that's me? Not bad. Sandy told me that I had a good bark. Junior asked me if I bark much on the trail. I told him I did not remember, but I don't think so. I really had to listen and you can't bark and listen at the same time. Can people do that? Talk and listen at the same time?

Mike tells me it is getting very late and he has to take me home. Mary, Sandy, and Mike need to leave Ray's place and head back to the city. Gee, I was having such a great time. Mike tells me that he will pick me up next weekend and bring me back to Ray's place. Okay that sounds like a plan.

Mike loads me into the travel kennel and we drive back to my home. He tells me that it is very dark outside, so he is driving slower to be safe.

Mike talks about some of the emails he received this week and has some bad news. One of my fur buddies went to the Bridge. I felt very sad, because this fur buddy had written to me. However, Mike said I should be happy that my buddy is now in a safe place, where she will not be sick any more. That made me feel better.

We arrived at my home and Mike walked me to my dog-house. He got some fresh water for me, and then stashed some biscuits in my doghouse. I jumped up and gave him a big hug and he told me to be a good boy. He will see me in a few days. Silently, I wished him good luck on his new job. He gave me a big body hug, rubbed my tummy and left. I heard him get into the truck and drive off.

A few minutes later, as Lakota and I were talking, the rest of my buddies came up the hill to my doghouse, and asked me what I did all day. They were all so happy for me because I had such a great time. They told me Mike had given them ear rubs and biscuits when he came to get me. They wished he could have stayed and spend some time with them before he left. However, it was getting late and it was very dark.

Then I heard Lakota yell, "What are you doing over there by Rivers' doghouse?"

I found these dog biscuits and now they are mine." Spot yelled back to us.

Nitro got up to challenge Spot, but I told Nitro just to let Spot have them.

"But Rivers," Nitro said, "Spot should not take what is yours. He is being a bully and just mean."

I told Nitro it was not worth fighting over a few biscuits.

I knew Nitro and Lakota were upset when they told me Spot left my doghouse. I led my friends over to the other side of the house and dug up a bunch of biscuits that Mike gave me. I shared them with all of my buddies. As my friends enjoyed their biscuits, I heard Spot grumbling by his doghouse. Then I felt Doc besides me. He told me to be careful, that Spot can be very mean when he does not get what he wants. I told Doc that I was not worried, I have nothing that Spot would want. Doc said I was wrong, I have friends, and Spot is jealous that I do. I thought about that and Doc is right, I do have friends, a lot of friends. Besides the team, there is Mike and Mary, Dr. Jim and Ray, Sandy and Junior. What about all of those nice humans and my fur buddies who wrote to me and helped with my operations? I guess for a little blind dog, I sure have a lot.

A New Dog House

What a wild week this has been. The rain poured and the wind roared all around us. The wind was so bad that I thought my doghouse would fly away!

Spot was being his mean old self again this week. He has been hanging around my doghouse knowing that Mike stashed some dog biscuits in there for me. Spot thinks I don't know he is there, but I can smell and hear him. I guess when I went blind; my other senses picked up the slack. Sure, nothing can take the place of having sight, but I bet I can smell and hear things better than other dogs. I also sense when things are near me. Mike calls this "radar." He noticed that while I can not see, I have a good idea as to things that are around me. He says I can probably "feel" things before they touch me. However, he also told me that when I get excited, I tend to go faster than my "radar" can pick things up.

Back to Spot. As I said, he was hanging around my doghouse looking for the biscuits, but I have them hidden. Anytime Spot comes near, Lakota or one of my other buddies calls out, "Hey Spot, what are you doing by Rivers' house?" He gets very frustrated and grumbles. The last time Spot was by my house he made some nasty comment that I was a useless dog since I am blind. He also said I do not contribute or have any worth. He called me a loser!

That really hurt and I was very angry with him. When Lakota came by with Nitro and Doc, they told me that I should pay no attention to Spot. He is just a grumpy old has-been, whose glory days are fading. He cannot handle the truth that the younger dogs are replacing him. Nitro said that Spot may have trouble making the team this year. He is getting old.

However, Spot's words did hurt and I did a lot of thinking about them. I sure wish Mike understood Bark. If he did, I could talk to him about this and see what he has to say.

A day or so after this, Terror came by to talk a little. He told me he heard what Spot had said. "So I guess you are just laying here thinking about all of the mean things Spot said."

"Yeah, I guess so," I replied.

Then Terror asked me a very strange question. "Why?"

"Why? What do you mean why?" I asked.

Now, Terror will probably be the lead dog for Mr. Raymie's team in the next big race from Anchorage to Nome. Terror is a great leader and I respect him a lot. "Didn't you run the race two times and you were blind during both races?" Terror asked. "Sure, but…" I replied, but he interrupted me with "Has any other dog on the team ever done that?" I thought for a minute, "I don't think so."

Terror then said "No dog on this team has done that and you should be extremely proud of what you did. You did not give up when one of your most valuable possessions was taken away from you. You are a very brave, strong and dedicated dog. You don't give up. Since you know all of that, why do you waste your time thinking about the dumb remarks of a grumpy old dog, a bully, really. Ever notice that Spot never says things really mean to any dog that would stand up to him?" I just nodded and Terror continued, "Spot picked on Doc constantly. Doc just ignored him, but finally Doc stood up to Spot and Spot stopped. Now he is trying to bully you. He knows you can't stand up to him because you are recovering from the operation, and Spot knows that he has a big advantage over you. He can see." Terror continued, "Spot is just a mean bully who thinks that being a bully is the only way he can be a leader. And he don't like Mike," he said.

"And here is one more thing for you to think about, my friend," Terror said. "I don't know if you will make the team or not. If you do, I would be proud to lead you to Nome." With that, Terror walked back to his doghouse.

Lakota overhead Terror's remarks and said, "Terror is right, Rivers, Spot's words mean nothing, unless you let them."

The rain and wind stopped, and I was just hanging around my doghouse when I heard that unmistakable "Yo buddy, how ya doing?" Before I knew it, I was in this big body hug and getting my tummy and ears rubbed all at the same time. I heard the click of the leash and I started to take off. "Easy Rivers, take it easy, we got all day." Mike said. He walked me (or did I walk him?) to his truck with the big box on back. I was so excited that I did not sense Mike's friend Ray, who started to rub my ears and tell me how good it was to see me. I heard Mike say to Ray that my eyes are looking better. Another week or so and they will be normal.

Mike lifted me up and put me in the big box on the back of his truck. Mike told me that they were going to give some biscuits to the team, and would be back soon.

I listened to both of them as they gave biscuits to the team, even Spot. I heard Mike talk to Lakota, Doc, Nitro, Brownie, Ugly, Terror, and the rest of my buddies while giving them ear rubs and scratching their backs. I knew they like that. I heard Spot grumble and both Mike and Ray laugh. "He don't change, does he." Ray chuckled. "Wait until Spot realizes that his son Junior will be trained to lead the team with Terror to Nome during the next race."

Did I hear right? Junior will be trained to be a lead dog! Terror and Junior may lead the team to Nome during the next big race! What great news! That will make me work harder to make the team.

Soon they returned and Mike started the truck and off we went. Where are we going? They forgot to tell me.

The smells coming through the open screened windows of the big box on Mike's truck are real familiar. I know. We are at Ray's house. I hear Junior and Sandy barking. Mike takes me out of the truck and leads me around a little and then to my big soft bed.

Mary is there also. She comes to me and gives me a big ear rub. She said my eyes are looking better each time she sees me. "And we got salmon and hot dogs for you, Rivers," Mary said. Wow, what a treat for dinner!

Mike tells me that they are building doghouses for Junior and me. Junior will be moving to my home for training and will need a new doghouse. Mike said they had some extra wood and were going to build me a new one too. Yes, I remember he told me that a few weeks ago.

Sandy and I were talking about Mike's new job and I did not notice that Mike, Mary and Ray left for a bit. When they returned, Mike has a treat for all of us. Something called a cow's hoof. Junior and Sandy must know what these things are. They started to chew on theirs right away. I started. Wow, is this thing hard! I would chew a little and stop. Whew, this is work!

While Ray and Mike were working they would call out to us, come over, give us ear rubs, and play with us. Mike would rub me up really good and I would jump around a little, but I was not sure where he was, since his scent was all over me. He would touch the tip of my tail and I would jump in that direction, but he was not there. Then he would touch my tail again and I jumped in that direction, but he was not there either. Then he just gave me this great big body hug and laughed.

He went over to Sandy and played with her while Ray would come over and give me a back rub. This went on all day. I wonder when they found time to build the doghouses.

Mike and Ray finished building the doghouses and Mary painted them. Junior could see them since he could look right into Ray's garage. "Hey Rivers," Junior said. "Want to know what our new houses look like?"

"Sure," I said, "Please tell me all about them."

He told me that they were on legs that raised them about six inches off the ground. Each one had a flat roof. The door was on the right side of the front so we would be out of the wind. Junior said that it was just the right size for us, and we would fit into them perfectly. He told me that Mary had painted them a nice yellow color. She also had painted a black sign with white letters on them. The sign on the first dog house had RIVERS painted on it and the other sign had JUNIOR painted on it.

My own personal doghouse! I never had one before. Junior said the paint was still wet so I probably will not get into it until tomorrow. Never mind that. My own house! Thanks guys.

I cannot see it, but I know I have new doghouse. I was just thinking that if Spot were right and I am so useless, why do Mike, Mary, and Ray treat me so good? Why do Sandy and Junior talk to me and treat me so well? Lakota, Terror, Doc, and Nitro are right. Just ignore Spot. He is just jealous!

I was so lost in my thoughts that I did not smell the food dish that Mike put in front of me. Then it hit me. Salmon, hot dogs, and what are these, bits of turkey. It doesn't get much better than this!

Well my belly was full. I think I laid on my bed and chewed on this cow hoof a little more. The last I remember before dosing off was hearing Sandy snore.

After a while, Mike came out, put a leash on Sandy and me, and told us we were going for a walk. Mary had Sandy and Mike had me. Ray went also.

I took off like a shot down the trail and Sandy tried to keep up. She pulled the dickens out of Mary. Mike reigned me in and told me to take it easy. Sandy was having a real hard time. I heard her breathing very hard, so I eased up. Soon we were all walking together and just having a great time.

When it was time to go home, Mike put me in the big box on the back of his truck. I had a great day and I really did not want it to end. Soon we were at my home and Mr. Raymie greeted us. Mike and Ray took my new doghouse out of the back of the truck and Mr. Raymie said it was sharp looking. The paint was still a little wet, so they said I would have to let it dry and I can use it tomorrow.

They all talked a bit. Mike got me some fresh water and took me over to my old doghouse. He told me that he would be by in a few days to get me and take me to his home in the city. We have to see Dr. Jim. Mike is going to get me early so that I can spend some time in his back yard. I can't wait!

Mike gave me a big body hug and a bunch of ear and tummy rubs, and told me he had to go. As I heard him walk off, I went into my old house. What is that I smell? It is that cow hoof. How did it get here? I started to smile as I laid down to chew on it.

"Hey Rivers" Lakota said, "How are you doing? Tell us about your day with Mike."

The gang all came around my house and we talked. I told them that the next time Mike came I would go to see Dr. Jim. If Dr. Jim gives me the okay, I can start training with the team.

Ugly said "Great, I have been practicing running straight instead of with my butt out to the side so I won't knock into you on the trail."

Nitro started to laugh and said, "Yeah Rivers, he has been practicing. We all have. We can't wait until you can start training with us."

We all talked a little bit more, and then it was time to hit the sack. Nitro and Lakota were the last to leave and told me that Mike had given each of them a special treat. It was very hard, but tasted very good. Did I know what it was? I told him and showed him what was left of the one Mike had given me. Nitro told me that Spot was very upset because he did not get one. I told Nitro that I overheard Mike talking to Ray and Mr. Raymie that Mike wanted four to six dogs to live with him and be his team. Not for racing, but just to go out on the trail and have a good time. I told them that Nitro and Lakota were two of my buddies that Mike mentioned. They said, "Mike likes us?" I told them, I think so.

With that, Nitro said that when he retires from racing, he would really enjoy being on Mike's team. Nitro said good night and went back to his house. Lakota told me that he hoped Mike would take him too. I hope so since Lakota is my best friend.

I curled up in my doghouse and pretty soon was dreaming of being a lead dog on the trail to Nome.

Retirement??!!

What a week! I moved into my new doghouse that Mike and his friend Ray built for me, and Mary painted. The gang came by to admire it and I gave them some of the biscuits that Mike stashes in there for me. Even grumpy old Spot came by. He made some snotty comment about me being a "pampered pet" with a fancy new house, and not being a racing sled dog any more. Sure, his words hurt, but I gave him one of my biscuits anyway. He took it, grumbled and walked away. Not even a thank-you! Wonder how he will feel when his son Junior gets here in a few weeks with his new doghouse, which is identical to mine!

Nitro told me that there is a sign on my doghouse with my name on it. Lakota told me it has a black sign with the word RIVERS painted on it in white letters. I told them Mary had painted it for me. Of course, when I told them about the great meals Mary cooks for me, they all said they wanted to meet her. They all liked my new house, and thought it was cool that I got a new one.

While they were by my house, we heard the honking of geese flying south. Doc said there must be 50 or so geese in that group. I think Teacher said that the snow was lower in the mountains, a sure sign that winter and snow will be arriving very soon. The gang headed back to their houses, but Lakota, Doc, and Nitro stayed with me. Nitro asked if Mike was coming and I told him he would be here soon, since he has to take me to the eye vet to get my final checkup and clearance to start training.

Nitro and Lakota told me that this might be their last year

for racing. "We are big dogs and the mushers seem to want smaller, faster dogs, not big powerful dogs like us." Nitro said. "Maybe Mr. Raymie will retire us. You know he is looking at smaller, faster dogs, like Junior. Yeah," Lakota added, "I am getting old and tired also. That Junior has so much energy. I get tired just watching him!"

Then Doc said a very odd thing, especially for a lead dog. "Maybe Mr. Raymie will retire me also."

"Wait a minute guys," I said, "What is all of this talk about retiring?" Nitro answered me. "Rivers, you are a strong dog, a smart dog. I have seen you run and you are very fast. You are all heart."

Then Doc added," But Rivers, there comes a time when you realize that no matter how good you are, there are younger, stronger and faster dogs, just around that bend, waiting to overtake you, and leave you in their dust."

Nitro asked "Rivers, who do you think will be Mr. Raymie's lead dogs in the next big race?"

Before I could answer, Doc answered for me. "It will not be me and it won't be Spot. We have been his lead dogs for many races. Remember," Doc continued, "younger and faster dogs."

I was thinking about this when Lakota asked me "What happens if you don't make the team, Rivers?" Shock time, I never thought of that. "Well I ah.... don't know, I...." I really did not know. How would I react? Then their words really hit home. Younger, faster dogs, who can see! Tough competition, but I have already made up my mind to do my best. If I do not make the team, I will always know that I gave it my best shot. Sure, I will be sad, but I did my best.

I was deep in thought when I heard Doc ask Lakota and Nitro, "Has Mike been giving you extra biscuits and ear rubs?"

"Why do you ask?"

Nitro replied, "Because he has been giving me extras and I notice he spends more time with us than he does with any other dog except Rivers."

Wait a minute. I heard Mike and Ray talking about Lakota, Nitro and Doc. Now what were they saying? Yes, I remember, Mike was wondering if Mr. Raymie would help him set up a small kennel. He was wondering if Mr. Raymie would let Doc, Nitro, Lakota and a couple of the other dogs plus me, live with Mike at his new home. Ray and Mike were talking about recreational mushing.

"Hey guys," I said, "What is recreational mushing."

Doc answered, "It is like racing, but you don't go as far and you don't need to go as fast. It is like taking a nice walk."

Nitro said "Many humans have dog teams just for that. They pack up some gear and head down a trail a few miles, maybe spend the night, and then come back home. I hear it is a lot of fun. Why do you ask?"

Now I did it. Should I tell them? Yes, they are my friends.

"You mean they were talking about us?" Doc asked, he was very excited. "That would be great."

Nitro said, "I bet that would be a lot of fun."

"Hey guys, don't get too excited or get your tails up." I said, "It is a long time until Mike moves into his new home, and keep in mind that Mike doesn't know how to mush, plus he has that bad knee. He may not want to."

"I bet that bad knee won't stop him." Doc said, "We can teach him to mush."

Then Nitro said "Hasn't he been using mushing commands with you when he walks you, Rivers, so you don't bounce into stuff?"

I was getting excited about this also. "You're right, he does, and I think I overheard him tell Mary that he was reading a lot of books on mushing, dog handling and setting up small kennels."

Well, we talked and talked. We were sure excited and it was very late when we all went to sleep.

Mike came early to get me to go to the eye vet. I know we had a long trip from the country to the city. His friend Ray was with him. I jumped up to greet Mike and he gave me a big body hug and ear rubs. He put me into the travel kennel and told me he was going to give the guys some biscuits. I must remember to ask Lakota, Doc, and Nitro tonight if they got any extras.

Soon we were on the road and I took a nap. All that talking last night made me a little tired this morning.

When I woke up, Mike was opening up the travel kennel and snapping on a leash. We were at his home. Yep, there is that big rock I like so much, and the tree, and the garbage can.

I remember the backyard. I heard the leash snap again. Mike

let me free and told me to go have some fun in the backyard.
I wandered all over the yard sniffing, and exploring.

When I finished exploring, I found Mike sitting on the deck.
I walked over to him and he stroked my head. He had a lot of
stuff to tell me about all of my friends who write to me. He
asked me if I remembered a little baby who was born prema-
turely. Yes I remembered. This was the baby who Mike asked
us to howl for. Well, Mike said that the baby was moved to a
new hospital and has a new doctor. The baby will require
some surgery to fix some problems, so I need to keep on
howling for her. Mike thinks the little baby was born on or
around the same day I had my eye operation.

Mike also told me about a friend of his named Dave, and
his dog, Pepe, who live in London. Dave makes hoops for
blind dogs. Mike explained that the hoop is attached to a vest
or harness. The hoop is about nose level and acts as a bumper,
protecting my head from stuff I would bounce into. Sounds
interesting, but I cannot wear that racing, can I?

Mike said that it would not work while I was racing or
working with a dog team, but it would work if I were walking in areas that I was not familiar with. Mike said that he
probably would ask Dave to make one for me when they
come on the market sometime next year.

Then he really surprised me. He told me he was consider-
ing getting a small sled and some dogs next year after he
moves. Mike said he wants to learn to mush dogs. He also
said that Ray may run a local 200 mile race and he will talk to
Ray to see if he will use me in the race. That would be great!

We talked about a lot of things. He said he was approached
on writing a book about me. A book about me! He told me
all about his new job and the nice people he works with. A
lot has happened this past week, a lot of news!

Then I heard Mary say "Hi Rivers, hungry?" Mary put the food
dish in front of me. Mike told me it had hot dogs, pork chops,
(no bones he says), and some dog food. This stuff is good.

Mike told me that he was going to snap on my very long
leader. He says he is going inside to get his lunch and then
we are going to the eye vet.

After I finished eating all of my chow, I did some more
exploring of the yard.

In a short time, Mike and Ray come out of the house, and put my leash on and took me back to the travel kennel. "Time to go see Dr. Jim, Rivers," Mike said as he put me into the travel kennel. Then I heard Sandy jump into the back of the truck. She said hello and told me my eyes were looking very good. She told me her neck wound had healed. We talked while Mike and Ray took us to visit Dr. Jim, the eye vet.

Sandy went in first and got a clean bill of health. Next, it was my turn. I was a little worried. Would Dr. Jim be there, and would he give me the okay to race?

Yes, it is Dr. Jim! He said "Hi" to me and then picked me up and put me on to the table. He tells Mike that my eyes look very good and all of the red should clear up in a few more weeks. He says I am doing very well. He is very satisfied with my progress, so much so that there is no need for any more follow-ups, unless Mike sees something wrong with my eyes. Dr. Jim and Mike start to talk about dogs, the big race, and the book Mike is writing about me.

Hey guys, did you forget me? Can I race?

Well, let me get their attention. I sat down and started to howl. Yep that worked. I guess my howling caught them both by surprise and they started to laugh. Dr. Jim put his nose right in front of mine and told me that I could start training right now if I wanted to.

All right! I can start training to race. So, please get me off this table and start my training!

Mike puts me back in the travel kennel after he said good-bye to Dr. Jim. What a great guy that Dr. Jim is. He took away all of my pain. I told Sandy the good news and she seemed to be very happy for me, or was it the dog biscuit I left in my travel kennel that interested her?

When we got back to Mike's place, we all decided to take a walk on the trail. So we headed out. I think I was leading and I heard Sandy ask me to slow down. Sorry, Sandy, I forgot that my legs are longer and I can walk faster than you can. We walked the trail. I remember this trail. We went a lot further than Mike had taken me on our first trips after my operation. I heard the crunch of the leaves under our feet and the rippling of the creek. What a great walk!

When we got back to Mike's house, Mike let me loose in the back yard. He played tag with me and started to wrestle with me on the grass. After we stopped, Mike sat with Ray on the picnic table, and I came over to them. Mike just kept rubbing my head while he talked. I felt like a nap, so I wandered over to the soft grass and stretched out in the afternoon sun. This felt so good.

I heard Mike and Ray start to laugh. I was rolling in the grass on my back. I do not ever remember doing that. But, it sure felt good.

In a bit, the food bowl came out of the house again, filled with hot dogs and salmon. Sorry guys, I am still stuffed from lunch. I just want to relax here in the back yard.

I guess I must have dozed for a bit, because I woke to hearing Mary say it was time to go. So, Mike put me in the travel kennel. I did not want to go and put up a fuss. Mike said that I must go back to Mr. Raymie's if I wanted to start training for racing. He told me there would be plenty of time for us to have great walks and talks, but right now, I had a job to do, and that was to train to make the team. Mike is right, but I really wanted to stay. Mary told Mike that she would put my chow into a bag and I could eat it later when I got to Mr. Raymie's place.

I heard them all get into the truck and off we went. It was a long drive home and I had a lot of time to think. Thinking is hard work. I fell asleep.

It was late when they got me to Mr. Raymie's' place. Mike walked me over to my doghouse. I heard the crack of dog biscuits being broken and knew Mike was stashing them in my doghouse. He scratched my back and gave me one huge body hug. He told me he would see me very soon. As I jumped up, he gave me another body hug. Then Mike knelt in front of me and put his hands on both sides of my face. He held me very close to his face. He whispered that just as it was hard for me to leave Mike's place, it is just as hard for Mike to leave me also. He said that time will fly and we will see each other again very soon.

After he left, I was just loafing by my doghouse. I was a little sad. I had such a great time today. Moreover, it is always a sad time when Mike leaves. I know he will be back soon. I can't wait.

Since it was late, most of my buddies were sleeping, but Doc, Lakota and Nitro came to visit. I told them all that had happened and the great news that Dr. Jim said I could start training. They were both very happy for me and glad I would be training with them.

I asked them if they got any extra biscuits today and they said they sure did, and lot of ear rubs from Mike. Nitro told me that Spot was upset because they got extra biscuits. Doc said that Spot got some extra biscuits also, but he just grumbled.

This tired puppy had a very busy and exciting day. It seems that besides my dream of racing in the big race, I have another dream too. My buddies Lakota, Nitro, and Doc share that one with me. I bet Mike has the same dream also.

The Dream

The baby was very sick and we were racing down the trail to get the baby to the first aid station. Mike was running the team. Doc and Spot were in lead, Ugly and Brownie in swing, Teacher and Nitro behind them, and Lakota and me in the wheel.

We only had to run a few miles on this trail. However, it had started to snow and the temperature was dropping. We finally got to the first aid station. We left the baby and her mother with the doctor. The helicopter was ready to go. I heard the doctor and the mother run to the helicopter. It took off, right over us

Mike turned the team around and we headed back home. We were making very good time, until we took the bend toward the downhill run. We headed straight into the moose.

I heard the brakes on the sled grabbing for the snowy trail as Mike yelled commands to Doc and Spot to move the team around the moose. The trail was too narrow and Nitro told me we plowed right into the moose. Lakota said there were four big moose and they started stomping the team.

I heard Mike unzip the sled bag and jump right in front of me. I heard a loud bang. Mike had a rifle and shot one of the moose. Lakota said that Doc, Spot, and Brownie were gone. But, Mike shot one of the moose and it went down.

There was another loud bang. Lakota said a second moose dropped, but it stomped Teacher, Nitro, and Ugly before it dropped. There were two moose left and only Mike, Lakota and me.

I heard another moose charge and one loud bang. I heard Lakota drop and howl in pain. "Lakota, Lakota" I called, No answer.

Mike was just to my left and I heard the ground shake as one of the moose reared up on its hind legs and came down on both of us. I heard another loud bang. He must of shot the moose point blank, but it was too late. I heard the moose stomp Mike, who must have caught the full blow and went down. I heard Mike fall, but I did not hear him.

The moose had hit me also, and I knew I was hurt. I also knew that the fourth moose would stomp on me. I waited for the blow. It came, as I laid down next to Mike, with my head on his chest. I did not hear his heartbeat or could I hear him breath. The blow came. Instant pain and I become very cold. I started to dream of walking the trails with my buddy Mike.

"Yo Sleeping Beauty, you gonna lay there all day?" Startled, I opened my eyes and saw Mike and the rest of the team in harness ready to go. There was fresh snow. Mike had a dark green harness in his hand with my name, RIVERS, in gold lettering on it. He also held a new collar, also green, also with my name on it.

Then I heard Lakota say "Rivers, look over here. It is me, Lakota." I turned head and saw him, and Doc, and the rest of my buddies. Wait a minute. I cannot see. I am blind what is going on?

I was very confused as Mike started to put the new harness on me. Before he did, Mike put his hands on both sides of my face and put his nose right next to mine. I was looking right into his face. "Hey buddy, you remember me telling you about Rainbow Bridge?" Sure I do. "Well, we are all here, we crossed the Bridge after the moose attack." Mike continued, "Remember I said that there are no sick dogs here? Well, Rivers, here you can see."

With that, he put my brand new harness one me. As I looked around, all of my buddies also had brand new harnesses and collars. They were the same color as mine and they had their names on them, just like mine.

Then Doc told me that we all had new doghouses and they each had our names on them. I looked around and saw them. Beautiful dog houses with decks and big fluffy pillows inside to sleep on. I saw mine. A big yellow house with a black sign with RIVERS painted on the front in big white letters. Lakota's house was right next to mine.

I noticed Spot walking over to me. In his mouth, he had his lead dog neckline. He dropped it at Mike's feet and said, "Why don't you and Lakota run lead for awhile, Rivers." I asked him if he was sure. He told me yes, he wanted me to be a lead dog also. Spot was being nice!

Mike finished putting me into the harness and he hooked the neckline up, so that Lakota and I were the lead dogs. Spot was behind me, teamed with Brownie. Teacher and Doc came next with Ugly and Nitro in the wheel. Nitro yelled "All right, lead dog Rivers, it is about time!"

With that, Mike said, "Okay team, get ready, let's go!" and with that, we raced down the trail leaving our tracks in the fresh snow!

"Hey Rivers, you are yelping in your sleep" It was Doc, Lakota, and Nitro standing at the door of my doghouse.

I opened my eyes, but I could not see. Lakota said I must have been dreaming because I had been twitching a lot.

A dream! It was all a dream. It was so real. I had to tell them the entire dream. They sat and listened. Lakota said, "That was some dream, Rivers. You remember all of those details? "Can you remember what I looked like?" Nitro asked. I told him. Doc said that the way Nitro looked in my dream was very close to what he looks like in real life. Then I told them what Doc and Lakota looked like in my dream. When I was done, Nitro asked me what color are Doc's eyes. I said blue. They told me I was right. Then I described what Mike looked like and asked them if I was right. They said that I was very close, but Mike is not as tall as you dreamed he is. However, he does have a beard.

We sat and talked about the dream and they were very interested in the Rainbow Bridge. I told them what Mike had told me. Doc said that he had heard stores about a place where dogs go when they got very old or very sick. It always scared him, but knowing about the Bridge makes him feel a lot better.

Time passed and before I knew it, Mike was there to pick me up. I jumped up to meet him and he gave me a bunch of hugs. Then he clipped on the leash and we were ready to go. Where? I really did not care. It is always so much fun to go with Mike. He picked me and put me into the big box on the back of his truck and he gave me some ear rubs and told me he was going to see the gang and give them biscuits.

Soon we were off. I took a nap. When I woke up, we were at Ray's house and I heard Junior say "Hi" to me.

Mary and Sandy were there also. After Mike put the long leader on me, I found my big soft bed and was ready to stretch out and enjoy a lazy day. Before I could, my food bowl showed up stuffed with hot dogs, salmon, and some chicken in it. Food first, stretching out later.

Mike and Ray were finishing up some projects around Ray's place. Every once in a while they would come over and play with me.

I guess they realize that I hear and feel their footsteps when they are near me. So they decided to play a game with me. They got on both sides of me and stood very quietly. Then one would jump up and down several times and I would turn toward that one. Then the other one would do the same thing and I would turn toward that person. Very soon, they were right next to me, rubbing and petting me. It was a lot of fun.

Sandy and I were a few feet apart. We had a lot of great conversations. Many times Mike would come over and pet both our heads at the same time.

When Mary came out, she rubbed the top of my head and told me how good it was to see me. I don't know why, but I jumped up to her, as I do with Mike and Ray. I never had done that before with Mary. She did not mind, just told me that I was a good dog. I am learning fast how to give affection to my human companions.

While Mike and Ray were working, Junior, Sandy and I were talking. I told them about my dream. Sandy said that it was very interesting because he heard Mike and Mary talking about doing some recreational mushing next year, and Mike wanted to buy a rifle to take with him on the trail. Junior said he overheard Ray and Mike talking about the same thing Junior mentioned that Ray was thinking of buying the same type of rifle.

Then Sandy really surprised me. She said that Mike and Mary were thinking of buying new green collars for us, with our names on them in gold lettering. She started to laugh and said Mike wanted to buy her a new green harness like the one he will buy for me and any other dogs that live with us after he moves, next year. "Can you picture me in a sled dog harness, Rivers?" She said. "I am just an old fat house dog that likes to mooch coffee from Mike's coffee cup!"

Junior started to laugh and said "Hey Sandy, I heard that they ran Labradors Retrievers in the big race to Nome. You are a Labrador right?" She was laughing so hard she almost could not answer. "You bet I am a Lab, a big yellow Lab, but I am no racing dog. I am a couch potato dog!"

We had a great time talking and telling stories all afternoon.

After a while, it was chow time again. They sure like to feed me. I was still a little full from lunch, but this was good stuff and I pigged out. The steak bone with some meat on it was just too much for me. Too bad I could not stash that in my doghouse for a late night treat, but right now, I am just stuffed.

I was just lying on my bed, enjoying my after meal snooze when Mike sat down besides me and started to wrestle with me. This was fun. He makes all kinds of funny sounds as he tickles my nose and plays with my paws. He tries to hold me down, but I wiggle out and jump around him. Soon we just sat together and he tells me all about the email we received last week.

I wanted to tell him about the dream, but he doesn't understand "Bark." He got very quiet for a moment and then told me that the baby that we were all praying for did not make it. She just could not fight any more, and now is at peace. Mike said she went to a place like the bridge for human babies.

I was very sad. I never met this baby, but through Mike and the emails, I guess we became friends.

Sometimes I wonder about all of these feelings I am having since I met Mike and Mary. I guess that the more we dogs are around our human companions, the more feelings we have. I must ask Doc about this feeling stuff. He will know. Maybe I should ask Sandy. She has been around human companions for a long time.

It was getting cooler and becoming very windy. I heard Mike say that it was time to take me back to Mr. Raymie's place. So I said goodbye to Sandy and Junior. Both told me they would see me next week. Mike took me for a fast walk so that I could mark the trail, and then put me into the box on the back of his truck.

Mike and Ray were in the front of the truck. I heard Mike open the window between the box and where they sat. That made me feel like I was part of their conversation. I could hear them talk.

After they got me home Mike gave me fresh water and showed Mr. Raymie the new food dish. Then Mike stashed a bunch of dog biscuits and cows hooves in my doghouse. He had given me one a few weeks ago and I really enjoyed it. He told me he would be right back. I bet he was going to Doc. Lakota, and Nitro's doghouses to give them treats.

After a few minutes, Mike came back, gave me a bunch of body hugs and ear rubs. He told me I was a very good dog and to have a great week. He said that he hoped I would start training this week. Last week it was too rainy to do any.

I jumped up on him and he just gave me another big hug. "Gotta go Rivers." He said. "See you next week." Then he was gone. I heard his truck drive down the road.

Before long, Nitro, Lakota, and Doc came up to my house. I had told them what had happen today. They told me that Mike gave them each a cow hoof and some extra biscuits. They also told me that Spot ran away for a few hours, but came home before it got dark. That was strange. Why would Spot take off like that?

It had been a long day and I was tired. My buddies left early and let me chew on the cow hoof that was in my dog-house. Soon I was dreaming again.

Another Visit

I was a little disappointed this week. I thought I would start training, but I did not. The weather is too warm and the training times have been cut back for all of my buddies. Guess Mr. Raymie is waiting for colder weather. Training, when it is warm or when the trail is muddy, can be tough and dangerous.

A day or so ago, Doc and Nitro came by my doghouse to visit with Lakota and me. They were very excited. They told me that there was a new lead dog to run on the B team. Spot may be going to be the B team as one of the lead dogs. This is news! Then Doc told me that he probably would not be running in the Big Race, but will be help train the younger dogs.

Doc seemed very happy with that. Nitro was also very excited. He said that he had been running lead during several of the training runs and he thinks Mr. Raymie was impressed. Since Nitro is so big, he normally runs in the wheel position to stabilize the team. Nitro was very proud of himself when he said, "Not bad for a six year old wheel dog!" I bet he had a smile a mile wide on his face when he said that. It is every sled dog's dream to be the lead dog. Few make it, so if you get the chance to run lead, it is indeed an accomplishment.

Doc asked Nitro who the other lead dog was that he ran with. "Terror!" Nitro said, "And is he fast and strong, smart too. He showed me a trick or two." Nitro added, "And what impressed me is that he wanted to teach me to be a lead." Doc said, "Well that is Terror for you, a true leader. I ran lead with him a couple of times," Doc continued, "And he just gets the team working together. It is fun to run with him."

I was very happy for my buddies. It seems they got what they wanted. Doc goes into semi retirement and Nitro get a chance to be the lead dog. Nevertheless, I was still disappointed that I did not get a chance to run this week. I guess Nitro picked up my mood.

"Rivers, something bothering you?" He said.

I told them that I really wanted to get back into training, but I did not run this week. Doc told me that it has been a very slow week. Mr. Raymie has been very busy with a lot of other things. That plus the warm weather is probably throwing his training schedule off. Doc said he was sure that I would get training time.

We talked about it and the time flew. Soon it was bedtime. I was wondering when Mike would come. I lost track of time this week. Now that is an odd thing for me to say. I don't tell time and since I cannot see, I cannot tell if is day or night. Sometimes, I can tell if it is daytime when the sun is out, and I feel it's warmth. Other times, I know it is night because it gets colder.

The nights have been getting colder, but I am nice and cozy in my new house. I have lots of nice soft straw. Moreover, don't forget my stash of biscuits. It is very nice in there.

Time passed and Mike did come and get me. For some reason, he parked down the hill from my doghouse so we had a short walk to get to his truck. My buddies started to bark a lot. I guess we were getting very close to their doghouses.

"You have a great time, Rivers." I heard Doc yell.

"Get a belly rub for me to, and enjoy yourself." Nitro said.

As Mike lifted me up into the box on the back of his truck, I heard Spot snarl, "There goes the pampered puppy. Going off to be a lap dog!"

I was angry. No sooner did Mike let me go into the big box than I jumped around and came right back out. But Mike caught me and said. "Easy Rivers, let me give your buddies some biscuits and then we will be on our way."

I guess he did not realize that I was very upset at what Spot said. I heard Terror say "Rivers, who has the friends? Who is going away for the day?" Who is respected? Is it Spot?" His questions stopped me and I thought about what he said. He was right. My anger faded away.

After my buddies, including Spot, got biscuits and ear rubs, we headed off. Soon we were at Ray's house and Mike told me that this was a "do nothing day." He told me that mean that we have no projects to do so we are going to enjoy a day off.

Junior and Sandy were there, and we all started to talk while Mike, Mary, and Ray went into the house. I heard the door open and Mike came out with my food dish and it had hot dogs in it! "Just a little snack for ya buddy, kind of hold you over until supper time." He said.

As he watched me eat, he told me that they were going to a mushers' swap meet. That is where the mushers go to buy, sell and trade equipment. He told me they would be back in an hour or so and when they returned, he would take me for a long walk. After I finished the hotdogs, I found my big soft pillow and stretched out for a nap. Sandy started to laugh at me and said that I sure like to nap a lot. I chuckled and told her that I remember that she also took a lot of naps and sunbathes when we were in her back yard together. "Sure did," She said, and soon I knew she was napping also.

I heard the vehicle pull up into the driveway and the doors open and close. It was Ray and Mike. They were very excited about all of the neat stuff they saw at the swap meet. They went inside and Mike came out a short while later. He clipped on my leash and took me for a walk.

I can not tell you how excited I was. I love to walk and run. I know I made a beeline for the gate and heard Mike laugh as he was running to keep up with me. Which way do we go? He let me go straight to the woods across the trail in front of Ray's house. I was just having a ball sniffing and marking.

Mike led me back to the trail and we soon started walking at a very comfortable speed. This trail had a lot of rocks on it. Mike was telling me about what he saw at the swap meet. He said he brought some booties so that Mary could make some for Ray. Now why would Ray want booties?

We made a left turn onto a new trail and it had that hard stuff called asphalt on it. Tough on the toes, but easier to walk a steady pace on. Mike told me Ray plans to run a local 200 mile race and wants to use me as a training dog. Ray may actually let me run in the race with him. That got my attention and answered my question about the booties.

I was getting excited again and picked up the pace. Mike said, "Easy, easy, you're not running any races yet, Rivers." With that, he reigned me in a bit. Next, Mike told me that he saw me in one of the Big Race movies. He said I was in the wheel position and looked like I was having a good time. He told me that I had a big smile on my face in the movie. Mike said that I looked very good, but he noticed I had the big "blue eyes" that I had when Mike first met me. Yes I remember that race; I went blind before that one.

This was becoming a very long walk. We made another left turn and must have been near the main trail because I heard a lot of noise. Mike told me that the noise was cars and trucks on a bigger trail. He said we were on a walking trail close to the big trail and we were safe. He wanted to walk about a mile or two down the trail to see some property he was interested in for the house he wants to build.

While I knew I was safe with Mike on the trail, I still got scared of all the noise from the cars and trucks. They sounded so close and there were so many of them. Mike must have noticed that I was not comfortable and said we would take another trail and head on back to Ray's house.

We made another left and got on another trail that had a lot of rocks on it. It was a nice, very peaceful trail. Mike was telling me about all of the nice people he met at the swap meet and about this one sled that impressed him. He told me that it was just the right size for him, four other dogs, and me. It was big enough to hold some gear for overnight camping. Sounds like fun. I can see it in my mind. Doc and Nitro would run lead with Lakota and me in the wheel. Maybe Brownie and Ugly would want to join us. While Mike says five dogs, I know we would need six. Now that would be a great team for Mike!

This is a very long walk, but I feel real good and strong. I have no idea where I am. I have never marked this trail. I hoped Mike knows where we are going.

I was really enjoying this walk and the happy thoughts I was having about Mike's sled team, when I noticed that Mike had stopped walking. I turned to "look" at him and he told me that we were in front of a house that was for sale. He said there was a pole with a box on it that had some papers in it describing the house. He read it to me. Sounds real nice.

Mike told me that the house has a fenced yard, a vegetable garden (carrots for Sandy) and there are a lot of woods behind it. He said he was going to look into it. I heard him fold the paper and put it his pocket.

The sun must have came out because it was becoming very warm. Soon we were back home and Mike put me back on the long leader. Mike must have known I was thirsty and wiggled his fingers into the water bowl so that I would know where it was. I drank a lot of water. After that I found my big soft bed and stretched out. Sandy and Junior asked how my walk was and I told them about the house and what Mike had told me.

I told them the house was near by and from what Mike said was a nice size house with a big yard. Sandy asked me if it was on a quiet street and I said it appeared to be, since I did not hear any cars driving pass us.

As we talked in the yard, Sandy made a comment about a movie that I was in. "You were in a movie?" Junior said in surprise. Before I could answer, Sandy said, "He sure was. Mike and Mary got the movie and we watched Rivers' part several times." After that, Junior asked me all kinds of questions about racing. Yep, Junior is one interested puppy when it comes to sled racing. I bet he will be a great racer.

Mike came out and gave us all biscuits and fresh water. Mike said that Ray, Mary and he were going out for a bit. When they return we would have supper. That sounds good, I was getting a little hungry. Nap time.

I smelled it before I heard Mike come out of the house with my food bowl. Hot dogs, salmon and bread with some warm water in it. It sure was good. While we ate, Mike told me that they were going out to eat and would be back soon. When they returned, Mary gave me a big chunk of country-fried steak. It was good.

Ray suggested that we all go for a walk. I was all for that. What really surprised me was when Mike put a harness on me. Are we sledding? I was very excited, but I knew to be very still while Mike put the harness on me. Once I heard the leash clipped on, I took off. I mean, I really took off to the point that Mike was having a very hard time controlling me. It took me a while to realize that I was not pulling a sled with my teammates, I was pulling Mike! Okay, okay, no sled, I'll take it easy. Even Junior remarked that he did not realize how strong I was. He told me I almost pulled Mike down to the ground.

Sorry. I just got carried away.

The rest of the walk was a lot of fun except for the big dog that crossed our path. We all stopped and both Ray and Mike yelled at it. I heard someone say "Come here" and Sandy told me the big dog moved out of our way.

When we got back to Ray's place, Mike took the harness off and started to wrestle and play with me. I was very worried that he would be mad because of the way I acted on the walk. I guess he realized how excited I was and how much I love to pull sleds. I hope they start my training this week. I know I am ready.

Our do nothing day was about to end. It was getting colder, and Mike put me in the big box on the back of his truck. Ray and Mike were in the front, and the window between the front and the back was open. I stuck my head though the opening and Mike petted my head and told me to sit down because he was going to start the truck. I did, and listened to them talk about dogs, mushing, trails, and their plans. Mike talked a lot about getting some dogs when he moves into the bigger house. If he asks me I'll come and live with him!

After we got to Mr. Raymie's house, Mike took me to my doghouse. I heard him put a bunch of biscuits and a cow hoof into my house. While he was getting some fresh water for me, some puppies came by followed by a big dog I did not know. While I was busy with the puppies, the big dog got into my house. I heard Mike yell at the dog and it took off, but every time Mike turned his back, the dog was there. Mike checked my house and told me the new cow hoof was gone. However, when he reached way back of the house, he found the hoof from last week.

He gave me a bunch of body hugs and told me I was a very good dog and he would see me very soon. I heard him talk to Mr. Raymie and they talked about my training. It would start this week. I heard them talk about Mike's plan to get some dogs when he moves and Mr. Raymie said he would help Mike with that. Mr. Raymie told Mike that he would teach Mike about mushing, so that Mike could mush with the team this year. All right, can I go, please, please?

After they left, Nitro, Lakota, and Doc came up and I had to tell them about everything that went on today. They were just as excited as I was. Nitro said that he heard Mr. Raymie and Mike talked about the same thing when Mike came to get me.

I gave them each a biscuit and we were munching on them when Spot and the big dog came up the hill. I offered them each a biscuit, but Spot said "no" and that they could take them from me anytime they wanted to. He was right. They could. But, I did not care. They could have all of the biscuits I have stashed away, that is, if they can find them. I can always get more because I have good friends.

The Ending to the Beginning

For the last few weeks or so, nothing much has happened. We got tons of snow and training was very intensive. Mike came and visited with me many times, but we seldom left Mr. Raymie's place. Mike got some mushing lessons and soon, he was taking teams out by himself.

I always ran with Mike's team. Sometimes Ray would run a team with Mike. Other times we would run three teams with Mr. Raymie running one team, Ray running another, and Mike and I ran the third. It was a lot of fun. I liked it the best when Nitro and Doc ran with Ugly, Lakota, Brownie, and me. Mike always ran fewer dogs in his teams since he was still new at mushing.

One day Mike came over to Mr. Raymie's house to get a team ready for a run. Mike said Ray would try to come over later with Junior.

Mr. Raymie said he was not feeling too well and for Mike to take six or eight dogs out for an exercise run. "Take Spot with you Mike, "Mr. Raymie said, "He needs to get some exercise and work with a different musher than me." Mike said, "okay" and started to harness up the team. Spot and Doc were in lead with Brownie and Ugly behind them. Next were Teacher and Nitro, while Lakota ran the wheel with me.

Nitro was upset. I thought it was because he was not in lead, but he told me that he had a gut feeling that Spot was up to no good.

I was thinking about what Nitro said when I heard Mike say, "Okay team, get ready, let's go!" and with that, we raced down the trail.

90

Mike does not run the dogs as fast as Mr. Raymie or Ray. He takes it nice and easy and works with us on pacing ourselves and working with commands. I heard Spot grumble about this run being too slow and he wanted to go faster. While we all can run like the wind, we follow the musher's commands.

We were on the top of this hill and started down the other side. Mike was trying to hold the sled to a nice, even pace, but Spot told everyone to start running faster. I heard the brakes grab and Mike yell "Easy team." Lakota and I started to slow down, but the team was moving too fast for us to make a big difference.

Then I heard Doc say to Spot, "What are you doing? This is too fast for going down hill. Slow it down, Spot"

He just snarled, "You old has-been, I am the lead dog and we go as fast as I say we go."

I heard Doc yell, "Look out" and then I heard a loud crack. Mike rolled the sled over on its side to get it to stop. We stopped very quickly and as we did, I heard Mike running in the snow to the front of the team

I heard a dog yelping in pain and asked Lakota what was happening. Lakota said the team's lines were tangled, and it looked like Spot was down. "Doc? Is Doc okay?" I asked.

Doc said, "I am okay, but Spot ran head first into a tree branch and he is down. No blood, but he looks really dazed."

Then Doc asked if anyone was hurt. The team was okay, except for Spot.

Lakota was telling me that Mike was kneeling over Spot to help him, but Spot was snapping and snarling at Mike. Doc said that Mike started to rub Spot's legs and body to see if there were any broken bones. "Take it easy Spot" Mike said, "I need to see if you are hurt." I heard Spot growl and Lakota told me that Spot jumped up and knocked Mike over onto Doc.

All of a sudden, Spot's growling stopped and he said he could not see. "What!" Doc asked.

"That tree branch hit me right across my eyes and head," Spot replied. "I can not see!"

Lakota said that once Spot stopped growling, Mike held Spot's face and looked right into Spot's eyes. "Well Spot," Mike said, "I don't know if you broke anything, but your face looks swollen and your eyes are very blood shot and closing. I think I am going to put you in the basket and get you home. I want Dr. Jim, to look at you." Lakota told me that Mike lifted Spot very gently and put him in the basket.

"Okay Nitro, you and Doc will run lead," Mike said while he was moving us into new positions. "Lakota, you and Rivers will run the wheel. Teacher you will run in a solo position behind Brownie and Ugly." With the dogs in new positions Mike yelled, "Okay team, get ready, let's go!"

The team raced back up the hill and down the trail toward home. We were really moving fast, a lot faster than we did before. I guess Spot's accident brought out the best in us. Doc and Nitro were leading the team over the trail just like the experienced racers that they are. All of us have raced, but this was different, Spot needed us. We kept going faster and faster, taking all of the turns and curves perfectly. I had to think about Mike. He never drove a team this fast before. I smiled to myself when I thought that he was doing pretty good for a rookie!

In no time at all we're back at Mr. Raymie's. Mike was tying the team up as Mr. Raymie came out of his house. Mike told him what happen. The next think I knew, Lakota was telling me that they wrapped Spot in blanket and Mr. Raymie put Spot in his truck and drove off to see Dr. Jim.

Mike came back and got us out of harness. He gave us fresh water and biscuits. He said he was very proud of us for the great way we handled Spot's accident and worked together as a team to get him home for help.

After a while, Mr. Raymie returned with Spot. Mike and Mr. Raymie moved Spot's doghouse up to where my house was. I overheard them talking. They said that the Dr. Jim found no damage but the blow to Spot's head caused him to go blind temporarily. It could last a day, a week but not more than a month. They said they moved Spot up near me because it would be easier to keep an eye on him.

When they brought Spot up, he just went in his house and laid there. After a while I told him I hope he was feeling better. He just grumbled. I offered him one of my biscuits and he just chewed on it, never even said thanks.

Later, I heard Spot get up and stumble into all kinds of things. "You okay Spot?" I asked as I heard him fall down after walking into something. "I can't see, I can't lead, what good am I?" He moaned.

He was feeling very sorry for himself when the rest of the gang came up to visit. They brought him some biscuits and other treats that they had stashed in their houses.

"Why are you doing this," he bellowed, "To make yourself feel good and gloat over my blindness?"

Lakota said, "You know Spot, for a lead dog, you really are stupid at times. No, we don't need to use your misfortune to feel good about ourselves, and we are not here to gloat."

Then Nitro added, "We are here because you are one of us, a dog, and we are a team. We stick together until the race is over."

Doc said, "Just because you are mean and a bully does not mean that we would not stand by you if you were hurt."

Then Spot said in a very soft voice, "I treated you very badly, Doc, yet you raced your heart out to get me home. And I was not nice to any of you, but you were there for me."

Lakota spoke up, "I think you are forgetting something, Spot. Your foolishness almost got us all hurt, but it was Rivers and Mike who really came to bat for you."

"What do you mean?" Spot asked.

"You don't remember that you started to race down that hill just to hurt Mike. You don't remember that after your accident, you snapped at Mike when he was trying to make sure you were okay. And it was Mike who picked you up, very gently, and put you in the sled basket. And don't forget Rivers. He did a great job to stabilize the sled in the turns and around corners to make sure you didn't get thrown out of the sled. Rivers constantly gave us encouragement and urged us on to go faster to get you home sooner. And what you may not know is that Rivers did all of this without a dog in front of him to guide him like we normally do. He could have eased up but he didn't. If he had tripped or faltered, the sled would have ran him over, ending any chance of Rivers making the team this year. He risked his own safety to make sure you got back home very quickly."

Silence. It become very quiet after Lakota finished. I could not see his face, but one of the gang whispered that there were tears in Spot's eyes. Then a very small and trembling voice said," I am so sorry Rivers, I am so very sorry." With that, Spot went back into his doghouse, but the sounds of his sobbing continued for a long time after that.

For the next few days, Spot and I talked a lot. I passed on some of the things I learned about getting around as a blind dog. Spot was a fast learner, and soon he could get around with out bumping into things.

One morning, I woke up to hear Spot yelling, "I can see! I can see!" He was very happy and he woke up all of the gang to tell them.

In a while, Mr. Raymie moved Spot's house back down the hill. However, Spot came up to tell me that he was so very grateful for my help when he could not see. He said he learned some valuable lessons. Then Spot came very close to me, told me I was a great dog, a great leader, and he will always be sorry for what he did to me. Spot asked if he could be my friend. I told him I would really like that. He gave me one of his biscuits and left.

A while later, Lakota, Nitro and Doc came up to my house and told me that the list was up, identifying which dogs made the team. They told me the names. They were sorry to tell me that my name was not on the list. I didn't make the team! I was very disappointed. Nitro said they was having a party for the team dogs, and asked if I would like to go. He would lead me and make sure I got back home okay. I told him I rather just hang around my doghouse. He told me I really should go, but I was not in the mood.

I guess when Mike came I must of really looked pitiful "Jeez, what a sad looking dog you are, Rivers." Mike said. "What's your problem?" He rubbed my ears. He put this big body hug on me. This hug seemed a little tighter and longer than normal. Was I just imagining that? Boy I wish he understood "Bark." I would really like to talk to him about how disappointed I was feeling.

"So you did not make the team," he said, "And that makes you feel sad?" He knew why I was sad! "Well there is nothing I can say that will make you feel better, but have you considered yourself to be a true champion? I bet not, Rivers, so let's look at some facts," he said.

Mike sat down next to me and put his arm around me as he continued. "First of all, ribbons and medals don't make a champion. It is what is inside of you, your courage, your heart, your attitude, your loyalty, and your love of others, that makes you a champion. A true champion is dedicated to be the best that he or she can be. You ran the Big Race two times. Not many dogs have done that. You were part of a team that saved Spot from going blind for good, and you put yourself at risk doing that. Not many dogs have done that either. Yep, not a whole lot I can say that will make you feel better. But let's take off for a bit, maybe a ride in the truck and some of Mary's cooking might cheer you up."

I heard him clip on the leash and off we went. This time he did not put me in the big box in the back of the truck. Mike put me in the front seat with him. "Time for you to be a co-lead with me on this trip, Rivers." Mike said, as he put some kind of safety harness around me. After a while, I just laid across the front seat and put my head in Mike's lap while he drove. He was talking to me, but I did not hear what he was saying. As he talked, he stroked my head and rubbed my ears.

The ride seemed longer this time. Guess I just lost track of time. When the truck stopped and Mike put me on the ground, I did not recognize any of the scents. Mike and I walked a bit and as we rounded this corner, I heard Lakota, Nitro, and Doc say, "Well it is about time you got here."

What is going on, I thought. Before I could ask, Mike was taking off my old collar and putting on a new one.

Then Sandy came up to me and said, "Welcome to your new home, Rivers."

Then Lakota said. "Yes, this is a real nice home we have here. We got new green collars with our names on them. We also have nice new green harnesses and our new sled is small and light, just great for recreational mushing with a small team."

Then Nitro told me that Brownie and Ugly were there too.

Brownie told me that we each had a doghouse with our name painted on it. There was a sign near the doghouses that said "Mike's Canine Resort. And there is more," Doc said. "We are all semiretired!"

"Mike is thinking about training us to be therapy dogs," Doc said. Before I could ask what a therapy dog was, Nitro told me. "A therapy dog helps sick humans. They play with us and pet us, because that helps them feel good and get well. It can be a real fun deal." He was very excited. But he was not finished. "Oh, by the way, welcome to the 'Howling Rivers Kennel'." He was laughing so hard he almost could not speak.

I was confused. "What is happening here?" I asked. Well Rivers," Sandy said. "Mike and Mary bought this nice house with a big back yard. Mike has been busy building new dog-houses for all of you guys and he brought the boys over this morning before he went to get you."

"Yeah" Ugly added, "We all had to keep quiet about this, so that you would be surprised."

Nitro said, "We are all now on Mike's team. And we can still go and visit the rest of the gang at Mr. Raymie's, and help train his younger dogs, but this is where we will live. This is our home!"

Home! It finally hit me. I have a new home with all of my friends and my own human companion to be with me. As that wonderful thought filled my head, I felt Mike standing next to me. I jumped up to hug Mike, but he must have been caught off balance. I knocked him down on the snow. I just cuddled up to him and could not stop licking his face, as he rubbed me all over my body.

It is true, blind dogs see with their hearts!

Part Two

After moving into Mike's Canine Resort, my life, and those of my buddies changed a lot. Yes I was disappointed that I did not make the team, but as Mike said, I had done that, not once but twice. So what would I gain by running it a third time? Sure, I would have a chance at being on a winning team, but I know that winning is not everything.

Nitro and I were talking about this and he summed it up for me. He told me that we have it pretty good here. We get plenty of good food (Nitro really likes Mary's cooking), we have a nice place to live, our beds are warm and we get plenty of attention from Mike. We get to run as a team. We also see our buddies at Mr. Raymie's place when we go to visit or help train his new dogs. "Rivers, we paid our dues, not it is time to relax and pass on our knowledge and wisdom to the younger dogs," Nitro told me.

He was right. When I think about it, it was only short time ago that I was a lonely sad dog, in a lot of pain. Now I am pain free, I have a warm, loving home, my friends are around me, and I got a great human companion who gives me a lot of affection and attention. I run with a team that works very well together, and we have a lot of fun doing what we love to do. It was what Doc said that really hit home. "We are not getting any younger, so let's enjoy the life we have left to live."

One day, Mike took us to Mr. Raymie's place to see our buddies and help train his new dogs. Mike made sure that our green collars and harnesses were clean. When we got to

Mr. Raymie's, Mike put our harnesses on us. Ugly told me that when we go to visit, we are a sharp looking team. That made me feel good. Brownie told me that Ugly really perks up when Mike puts his new collar and harness on. "You can tell Ugly is really proud of his new gear." Brownie would say.

After we got to Mr. Raymie's, Spot came up to me and asked me how I was doing. He sure has changed. He really is a nice guy. He told me that he loves to have us visit because we help the younger dogs out so much. They really respect us, he said. Spot was very happy because he found out that he would be the lead dog on the "B" team in the Big Race. That is just great, I told him. I was very glad that he got his lead dog position back.

"Terror is having some problems with a couple of the new dogs on the 'A' team" Spot said. "One in particular, Smokey Joe, is a real bad dude. He wants to be a lead dog, but doesn't have the ability." Terror is trying hard, but Smokey Joe just wants to fight. I am not sure why Mr. Raymie wants to use him. Sure, Smokey Joe is big and fast, but he is not smart. Someone said that this is his last chance. If he don't work out, well, he won't be staying here for too long. I think Mr. Raymie has been asked to train him." Spot finished by saying to me, "Be careful around him, Rivers, he is a real mean bully, and will pick a fight for no reason at all." With that Spot went back to the dogs in the 'B' team and started some training.

I was just standing there thinking about what Spot had said, when suddenly I felt this big dog bump into me. "Hey runt, why don't you look where you going," a voice yelled in my direction. "Excuse me," I said, "I was just standing here...

"You calling me a liar, runt?" the voice said, interrupting me before I could answer.

Then I heard Lakota, Teacher and Nitro walk up to me and Teacher said "Hey Smokey Joe, what are you doing with Rivers?"

"So," Smokey Joe said, "This is Rivers, I heard about you. You don't look like much."

Then Nitro said, in a very mean voice I had never heard him use before, "Rivers is my friend. In fact he is a friend to all of Mr. Raymie's dogs, and he has proven himself. You start to pick on him, you will answer to me and every other dog here. And don't forget that you will have to deal with Mr. Raymie and Mike."

I heard Teacher, a good size dog, who was standing right next to Nitro say, "If you are looking for trouble, Smokey Joe, you definitely have found it."

Before I knew it, all of my teammates were standing next to Nitro, Teacher, Lakota, and me. This was getting very ugly, so I said, "Look, Smokey Joe, we want no trouble. If you said I bumped into you, I am sorry. I don't "see" very well. I hope you will accept my apology."

"Yeah," he said, "but don't let it happen again." and then he walked away.

We were all just standing there discussing what had just happen when Mike came up and said "Looks like you guys met Smokey Joe. Mr. Raymie told me about him. Bad news." Mike said, "I saw what happened. He purposely walked into you, Rivers. So how about if you just hang with me, and let Smokey Joe go his own way. I understand he has been a problem on other teams. If he doesn't want to be trained, then we won't train him."

Then Mike said, "okay guys let's, get back to work."

A short time later, we heard many of the dogs start barking. I head some growling also, and then Mike said. "It is Smokey Joe tangling with Rex." Rex and Smokey Joe, Oh no! Rex is 17 years old. He is the oldest dog at Mr. Raymie's place and was his lead dog for many years. I heard Mike start to run and yelled "Stop it!" at the dogs. I hope there is not a fight. Rex is no match for Smoky Joe.

As Mike tied my walking leash to something to keep me from getting into the fight, Lakota came up and told me that Nitro and Teacher are protecting Rex from Smokey Joe. "You are not going to believe this." Lakota said, "but Mike just picked Smokey Joe up off his feet and walked him, to the other side of the yard." We head Mike yell "Stay" to the other dogs and they quieted down.

I heard Mike clip a leader on Smokey Joe. We all heard Mike talk, as Smokey Joe just hissed and growled at Mike. "You will not fight in this yard. You will not bully the other dogs. You will not start any trouble. If you do, I will keep you on a leader far away from the other dogs. You will not get any treats either. You understand me, Smokey Joe? I hope you do and change your evil ways, or else you will be a very lonely and unhappy dog here. Just look around here and you will notice that these dogs work together as a team. They get along just fine, with no problems."

"I saw what you did to Rivers before," Mike said. "We do not tolerate your kind of behavior in this yard. And I won't put up with any dog causing trouble with any of my dogs. You have been warned, Smokey Joe. Do not cross me again."

There was an eerie quiet in the yard as Mike spoke. We have never heard him talk like that before. Lakota whispered to me that every dog was watching Mike as he talked to Smokey Joe. Moreover, Smokey Joe was listening! Besides stopping his growling and hissing, Lakota told me that Smokey Joe's ears went down and he started to cower, a sign that a dog is scared that he did wrong.

Lakota told me that Mike walked back to Rex. There was not a sound in the yard and I bet every eye was on Mike. Lakota said that Rex was lying down with Nitro and Teacher standing near him. Lakota said that Mike knelt down next to Rex. "Well you old Geezer, it looks like you got lucky and did not get hurt," Mike said. "You know there is no fighting in this yard, but I bet you got picked on. Smokey Joe is a very big dog, Rex. You have nothing to prove by tangling with him. You could have been badly hurt." Lakota said Mike gave Rex a bunch of ear rubs, and Rex got up, walked around and seemed to be okay.

Then Lakota said Mike turned to Teacher and Nitro. Lakota told me that both dogs sat as Mike talked to them. I heard him say. "So what do you two have to say about this? Let me guess. You saw Rex getting picked on and came to his defense. Now you boys were not looking for a fight were you?" You could hear the smile in Mike's voice as he said. "Nope, I bet you were just watching over Old Rex. Okay, I buy that this time, but I want you, especially you, Nitro, to stay way from Smokey Joe unless you are with me. You guys understand?"

Lakota told me that both Teacher and Nitro sat with their ears down while Mike talked to them. They knew Mike was serious, yet he was giving Teacher and Nitro the benefit of the doubt here. I bet this thing with Smokey Joe is not over yet. He may not cause problems when Mike is around, but I am sure that when we go home, Smokey Joe will be up to his evil ways.

I head Mike's footsteps as he walked back to Lakota and me. "We're going for a sled ride," Mike said as he put us in harness and hooked us up to the sled. Doc was next to me and told me that Nitro and Lakota were in the lead dog positions. Brownie and Ugly were next, followed by Teacher and a dog named Rudy. Doc and I were in the wheel position. I do not ever remember having Doc run Wheel with me. Doc must of read my mind and said. "Hey Rivers, I never ran Wheel before. This looks like it might be fun."

With that Mike yelled, "Okay team, get ready, let's go!" and with that, we raced down the trail, leaving our tracks in the snow!

Halloween

What a great training run we had. It was not very cold. It was fun to run on the fresh snow on the trail. Mike does not run us very fast, more like a fast paced walk. He tells us there is no point in rushing since we are not racing, but just out to enjoy the trail.

I like it a lot, and so do the rest of the guys. Just the other day, Nitro was telling me that he likes this gentler pace, and gets to see things on the trail that he never noticed before.

Doc also made a comment that he likes the breaks after a mile or so. We get to stop, relax and I think the guys enjoy the abundance of ear and tummy rubs Mike gives us.

Lakota, along with Brownie and Ugly, told me that they like it that because we are not in a rush to get some place, as is the case in racing.

Of course, we all get a little bummed out when Mike pulls us off the trail to let another team pass us. That really is not what bums us. It is the young pups and their "Old Geezer" comments that burn. We all would just like to run them into the ground. "Old Geezer," yeah sure. We all can run like the wind. Our age has nothing to do it. You have to have heart to be a racer, a champion. Didn't Mike tell me that?

Mike's "Whoa team" brought me out of my thoughts. We were home. Yeah, home, great chow, a nice warm soft bed, and all of the attention. Who cares what some young pup says? Nitro is right, we proved ourselves, and we have nothing more to prove. However, just once, I would love to race again, and show those young pups what a blind Old Geezer can still do!

From what Lakota has told me, our dog homes are located in a fenced-in part of the back yard, just behind the big house. It is very peaceful back here.

Mike had just finished taking our harnesses off when we heard Sandy bark and then Mary scream "Oh you scared me."

Then it was Lakota, saying, "Mary is in trouble, she needs our help," as I heard him and the team run off to help Mary.

I turned and started to run too, but then I heard Mike start to run also. I was running next to him and then I heard Mary yell "Stop." I heard all my buddies just stop in their tracks.

Then Mary yelled "Sit" and I heard them all sit.

When Mike and I got to where Lakota and the guys were, I asked Doc what had happen. Doc said that there was a funny looking creature on the front porch, in front of Mary

Funny looking creature? Then I heard Mike just start to laugh. What is so funny? This creature is attacking Mary. We have to do something. I started to move toward where I thought the creature was, but then I felt Mike hold on to my collar and say "Easy, Rivers, it is just Missy from down the block dressed up for Halloween." Halloween? What is that, I thought. I just sat down to listen to what was going on. This is very confusing.

I heard a voice say "Gee Mike, your dogs scared Missy and me, charging around the side of your house like that."

"I'm sorry, Marty," Mike said, "We just got back, and they heard Mary's scream when Missy came Trick or Treating. I guess they thought Mary was in trouble."

"Besides, my dogs would never hurt Missy, Marty. They know her. Sometimes we see Missy on the trail when she is coming home from school."

"Missy," Mike said, "how about coming over here and give these guys a little TLC? Let them sniff you, so that they know who you are. They don't recognize you in your Halloween outfit. But watch your goody bag, these hounds like treats."

I heard Missy come over to us, and Doc told me that the little girl started petting Lakota, and he was really enjoying the attention. Doc told me that she put a big hug on Lakota and told him he was cute. Doc told me that Lakota just nuzzled next to her.

"Well Missy, seems like you got a friend there," Mike said. "He is such a nice dog. What is his name, Mr. Mike? "Well, honey, his name is Lakota and he is a very shy dog, but he seems to be warming up to you. I never saw anyone get that close to him before. Let try something," he said. "I have been trying get him to come to me when I have a biscuit in my hand, but he seems very hesitant. You want to try?"

Sure Mr. Mike." Missy said.

Now I know Mike keeps biscuits in his jacket pocket and I heard him get one out and give it to the young girl. "Now Missy," Mike said," I want you to take about five paces backwards away from Lakota. Lakota, stay," Mike said as Doc told me that Missy started to take the five paces backward.

Nitro came up besides me and said "Rivers, this is amazing, the little girl is holding the biscuit out toward Lakota and asking him to come to her. Lakota is creeping toward her."

Wow!" Nitro said, "Lakota gently took the biscuit from the little girl's hand and now she is petting him again. I can't believe this. Lakota is licking her! He never does that."

"Well you are not going to believe this either," Doc added, "but Lakota is sitting in front of the little girl and just raised his paw for her to shake it. Now he just laid down and rolled over so she could give him tummy rubs. He never does that."

"Well Missy" Mike said, "looks like you just helped my big shy dog enjoy some attention. Anytime your folks say it is okay, you can come by and visit Lakota. Just make sure Mary or I are home, okay?"

"Thanks, Mr. Mike. I would really enjoy that." Missy said.

"You're welcome, honey, just give us a call to make sure we are home."

"I really appreciate that Mike," Marty said "Missy always wanted a dog, but we can't have one. Besides not having the room for one, Missy's mom is very allergic to dog fur."

"Well Marty," Mike said, "Missy can come by anytime that we are home and I have this feeling that Lakota would just love seeing her. I bet he would really like to pull her in the sled basket sometime. Maybe we can do that, if it is okay with you, Marty."

"That would be just great, Mike. Well it is getting late and Missy has school tomorrow."

Mr. Marty and Missy left, after saying their good-byes, and Missy giving Lakota one last hug.

104

Mike told us to go back to the yard. It was chow time. When we got back to where our dog homes were, I heard him kneel down by Lakota. Brownie was next to me and told me that Lakota was not acting shy, as he normally does, but sat right in front of Mike while Mike petted him and talked to him.

I heard Mike tell Lakota that he was very glad that Lakota was getting over his shyness and not to feel bad because he led the team to the front of the house and scared Missy. Mike told him that he was proud of Lakota for rushing to help Mary. Brownie said that Lakota's ears really perked up when Mike said that! I bet that made Lakota happy. Brownie said he was actually smiling.

Brownie said that Lakota rolled over so that Mike could give him a tummy rub. This was not the Lakota we knew. The best he would let Mike do was a few ear rubs. Tummy rubs, good going Lakota! "Say big guy." I heard Mike say, "this is something new for you, tummy rubs! Okay, how about a body hug also?" Brownie told me that Lakota just let Mike give him all kinds of tummy rubs and hugs. Brownie said that Lakota just kept on smiling and was really enjoyed himself.

After Mike fed us and gave us our nightly treats, Lakota came by my home and wanted to know if he could talk to me.

"Sure," I said, "What's up?" We have been friends for a long time, and I knew something was troubling him. Lakota hesitated for a moment and then asked me how I felt the first time I met Mike. I told Lakota that I was not sure what he was getting at. He asked me what is it like to really like a human.

That took me back a little. What is it like to like a human? I asked him if he liked Mike. "I think so." Lakota said. "I know he won't hurt me and he takes good care of me. I like it when he pets me and talks to me, but is that liking him? Besides," Lakota said, "he is your human and I don't want you to get angry at me if he gives me a lot of attention."

"Hold on." I said, "Why would I get angry if Mike gives you attention? I am glad that Mike gives you attention. Mike is not mine. Sure we are close and he is my special buddy. But I don't get upset because he shows you or the other guys attention." I continued "Mike likes all of us and he belongs to all of us. He has told me that we are all special to him. I will admit he gives me more attention because I can't see, but he gives all of us attention. He spends a lot of time with you, doesn't he, Lakota?" I asked.

"Yes he does." Lakota replied. "Maybe I am wrong."

No," I said, "just confused. I was just as confused when I started to work with Mike. It is different living here with only a few other dogs and humans giving you plenty of attention, than it is to live in a yard with 100 other dogs."

"But that is not answering your question about knowing if you like someone." I said. "I guess you know when you feel good around that human, and you want to please him. And, you feel bad when you don't or you are not around him. Does that answer your question, my friend?" I asked.

"I think so, but it sure is confusing being this close to humans." Lakota answered.

Then I asked him, "You sure were friendly and playful with Missy tonight once you realized she was not some strange creature."

"Yes," Lakota said, "I really enjoyed playing with her. I felt that I could be friendly and she seemed to enjoy giving me all of that attention. I sensed she needed me."

"I know Mike likes giving you, me and the rest of the team a lot of attention also." I said. "Missy probably needs a buddy like you. She cannot have a dog, but she can come here and be with you anytime Mike or Mary are home."

"Do you think she will come back to play with me, Rivers?" Lakota asked gently.

"I think so," I said.

Lakota thanked me and said it was time for sleep and headed back to his dog home. I bet he was smiling as he walked back. Lakota is older than me, and never had a human companion. I will howl for him that Missy does come back to play with him.

Missy and the Bear

Many times after our Hallow-
een adventure, Missy did come back to visit with Lakota and
the rest of us. As soon as I heard Missy, her dad, and Mike
talking, I could not help but hearing Lakota's tail start to wag
very fast. He was very excited. I know the feeling. I can remember how happy I was to see Mike when he used to visit
with me before I came to live with him.

As the three of them walked closer to our kennel area, I heard
Missy's dad say that he received a report about a rogue bear in
the area. He was telling Mike to make sure that there was no
food or garbage lying around, since that would attract bears.

Mike assured him that the garbage is kept in covered garbage cans in one of the sheds, while the food is stored in
covered containers in the warming shed." As you can see, Marty,
the kennel has two fences and I don't leave food around."
Mike said. "I clean up as soon as my buddies here are done
chowing down."

"Looks good," Mr. Marty said. "I would appreciate if Missy
stays with you and Mary today. Until this bear is caught, I
would hope that you would not be taking any sled rides." Mr.
Marty said.

"Not with a bear roaming around," Mike said. "Tell you what,
Marty. I got a bunch of chores to do around here so how about
if I let Missy play with Lakota and the other dogs in the fenced
in kennel area?"

"That sounds great. I know Missy would love to spend the
day with Lakota." Mr. Marty told Mike. "Her mom is not feeling
well and I have to work and track this bear. You don't mind if

Missy stays for the better part of the day?" Mr. Marty asked. "I will be back at around 5."

"Not a problem." Mike answered, "I am sure she will have a great time with Lakota. See you later, Marty."

"Okay Missy, you are going to stay with Mr. Mike and the dogs until I come back for you later today. Be a real good girl okay? With that bear roaming around, Mr. Mike will not be taking your for any sled rides and you will be staying in the kennel area with Lakota. Is that okay with you?" Mr. Marty asked Missy.

"That is just great, Dad. Thanks. I promise to be good." Missy said. Lakota, who was standing next to me by my doghouse, said that Missy's father knelt down and Missy gave him a big hug.

I heard Mr. Marty's truck drive off and heard Mike and Missy come near our kennel area. Mike said to Missy, "Please make sure you close and latch the gate. Sometimes these guys like to wander outside the fenced area, especially Rivers. For a blind dog he can wander off like the best of them." Mike said with that laugh he has in his voice when he is teasing me.

I heard Lakota sit down by my dog home, but as soon as Missy said "Hi Lakota!" All I heard was the sound of his paws running in the snow toward her. Brownie was laughing when he came over to my dog home. He told me that Lakota just rolled over on his back like a big puppy and Missy was giving him a bunch of tummy rubs. Doc joined us, and said that it was very good to see Lakota, who is a big dog, roll around like a puppy, and play with Missy.

Missy played with all of us. Sometimes we would go in to the warming shed and play in the straw. Other times, we stay outside and play in the snow. We were having a lot of fun. It was nice to have a young person around us. Missy has so much energy and likes to run and play with us.

I heard Mike chuckling as he was standing by my dog home watching us. I heard Mike say that he was going back to the big house to get some treats for us, and some lunch for Missy. I heard the gate open and close. I also heard Mike's footsteps fade as he walked to the house.

From what my buddies tell me, the kennel area is very big. On one side is the warming shed and the other is the shed where Mike parks the trucks. Between the two sheds is our fenced in kennel area. The fences are attached to the sheds. One fence, with the gate, faces the big house where Mike, Mary, and Sandy stay, and the other fence faces the woods. I have walked all over the yard and there is plenty of room for us to play in. Ugly told me that the fences are tall enough to keep moose out.

We were all playing and having a lot of fun, but what was that smell? I stopped playing and sniffed the air. Ugly asked me what I was doing and I told him I smelled something different. "I smell it also." Ugly told me. "I know that smell, It is bear!"

The wind shifted and I could not tell what direction the smell was coming from. Then I heard it. The footsteps of a very big bear are very scary for a dog to hear.

"Hey, guys," I said, "we got a problem." However, before the guys could answer, we all heard the roar of the bear as he came out of the woods to the back fence of our kennel area.

After the roar, it became very quiet. Then I heard Lakota and Nitro run to the fence and start barking at the bear. Ugly and Brownie joined them. I told Doc that we needed to get Missy into the warming shed where she can hide in case that bear came over the fence.

"Okay," Doc said, "you grab one of her coat sleeves and I will grab the other and we will lead her into the shed."

Missy was crying, scared, but she seemed okay when we grabbed her coat sleeves. Doc let the way into the shed. Doc told me there is a ladder for a shelving unit that is about eight feet off the ground. We can get Missy up there and then knock the ladder down so that if the bear gets into the shed, it can't get at her.

Doc let Missy to the ladder and she figured out what we wanted her to do. Once Doc told me that she was safe on the shelf, we both got behind the ladder and pushed it away from the shelf. Missy understood what we wanted to do and helped push the ladder away from the unit.

After we heard the ladder fall to the ground, Doc and I rushed back outside. Lakota was the loudest barker out there. I could not believe the growling and hissing he was doing. Doc told me the bear had come up to the fence. He said the fence was taller than the bear, but the bear could climb it if he wanted to.

Doc told me that the other dogs were facing the bear and barking at it. We came up behind our buddies and starting barking also. Doc told me that every time the bear started to climb the fence, Lakota or Nitro would jump up and snap at the bears' paws as they griped onto the chain link fence.

The bear was getting nastier, but we were determined that it was not going to come over that fence. I know that if that bear came over that fence, it could wipe us out. If that bear hits us with one of his big powerful paws, well, I don't want to think what would happen.

All we could do was try to keep it from coming over that fence. I heard the bear shake the fence and roar some more. Yes I know we all were scared, but we would not back down. This is our home and we have a friend here that we will protect.

It seemed like forever but it could not of been. I did not hear his footsteps but we all head the command, "Back, back!" Mike yelled. What does he want us to go back for? I thought. We must keep this bear from getting over the fence. Mike is no match for this bear. Again "Back, back," and then followed by "Down."

I heard my buddies back away from the fence and the start to lay down. Doc looked at Mike and told me he was in the kennel and he had his rifle. That is why he wants us away from the fence and lay down, so that he would not shoot one of us by accident.

While there was a lot of growling and hissing, we did not bark. Nitro and Lakota were on each side of me and told me that the bear looked confused because we stopped barking and backed away from the fence.

"He is coming over the fence," Lakota said, as I heard him get up.

"Down!" Mike said and Lakota laid down again.

Bam! I heard as the first shot rang out. Nitro said that the shot went between the bear's legs. A warning shot!

Lakota said the bear seemed confused but was still trying to climb the fence.

Bam! Bam! Two more shots rang out and I felt the ground shake as the bear fell to the ground.

A vehicle pulled up into the driveway, and I heard several footsteps running toward our kennel area. "You okay? Were is Missy?" It was Mr. Marty.

Then Mike asked, "Where is Missy?" All the dogs started to look around, as I grabbed Mike's sleeve and pulled him toward the warming shed. I heard Doc start to bark. It sounded like he was standing in the doorway of the shed. I heard Mr. Marty follow, as did the rest of the guys.

"Missy, Missy!" Mr. Marty called out. "Up here, Dad." Missy called down from the top of the shelving unit.

"You okay, honey?" Mr. Marty said.

"Yes Dad" She answered. "You will never believe what happened. When the bear came to the fence, Lakota, Nitro, Ugly and Browning charged the fence, barking at the bear. Doc and Rivers grabbed me by my sleeves and led me into the shed. Once I got up the ladder, they started to push it away."

"Is Lakota okay, Mr. Mike?" She asked.

"Well Missy, I think the big guy is waiting for you outside this shed."

As Missy saw Lakota she rushed to him and put a big hug on him. "You were so brave Lakota. So were the rest of you." She gave each of us a bunch of ear rubs. However, it was Lakota who she just hugged and hugged. .

"It is amazing how they protected her, Mike." Mr. Marty said. "It makes you think. Maybe they are smarter than we give them credit for."

"Yes, that is true, but I think it is more instinct." Mike replied. "They protect their musher or those weaker than they are. I have noticed that they will all gather around Rivers and make sure he is okay." I think they know he is at a disadvantage, and they try to help him. In this case, I think they knew Missy would be hurt and their natural instinct to protect the weak took over. To them, you, I and Missy are just two legged dogs."

"How did you know the bear was here?" Mike asked. "We tracked it to about a mile of your place and lost it." Mr. Marty said. "When we heard the dogs start to bark, we figured you had a problem. So we rushed over here. Looks like you took care of the problem."

Mike answered, "Yes, I really wish I did not have to do what I did, but I had no choice. The bear was determine to get into the kennel area. The dogs and the warning shot did not scare him off. He left me no choice."

Then Mike said, "Well let's take care of the bear. I know some heroes that deserve some extra treats and a special young lady who wants to give those treats to them."

As much as he likes treats, I think Lakota is too interested in the attention he is getting from Missy to care about treats right now.

Rivers and His Christmas Gift

Lakota told me that Mike and Mary had decorated the house with lights and decorations of snowmen and a chubby guy in a red suit. Nitro joined us and said the chubby guy had a big sled pulled by eight huge animals. Nitro said they looked like moose, but weren't. They had bigger antlers. Ugly came up to us and told us the moose-like creatures were reindeer. He has seen a herd of them when he lived up north. We were all wondering what was happening.

Mike came out of the house with our evening chow. It sure smelled good. As he filled our bowls with hot food, he was telling us that this was Christmas Eve. He explained what Christmas was all about. Mike told us that this is a season of giving and loving our neighbors, because we are celebrating the birthday of a very special person. In celebrating this special person's birthday, we give gifts to each other. Mike said we also decorate our houses as part of this celebration.

He told us that we were his special friends and he gave each one of us a big cow hoof as a Christmas present. With the present, Mike gave each one of us a lot of attention. Of course, Mike made me wait to last. As he gave me my present and ear rubs, I heard Mike toss extra biscuits into my doghouse saying, "here is something extra for my very special buddy." With those words, he gave me a very huge body hug. Then he told us that tomorrow, being Christmas, he will load up our sled with some gifts and goodies, and we will deliver them to some people who really need a Christmas gift.

Soon the gang was asleep in their doghouses, but I was

restless. Mike's words troubled me because I had no gift to give him. He has given me so much and yet... Maybe I just think too much for a dog. The other dogs do not seem to be thinking about it. Maybe Sandy will know the answer. I will ask her tomorrow.

It was a quiet and peaceful night. There was a fresh dusting of snow on the ground. I could not sleep.

I decided to get up and walk around the yard. We live in a fenced in yard, and after living here with Mike and Mary at their new home for while, I am very familiar with the yard. Mike calls this the "community yard" where we all gather for our meals and some training sessions.

Lakota told me that on one side of the yard there is a building where Mike parks the trucks. On the other side, Lakota said, was the warming hut. Mike takes us in there to care for us when we are not feeling well. Sometimes, if it is too cold he will let us sleep in there. While we Alaska Huskies like the cold, it is nice to go indoors every once in a while. Many times Mike takes us in there just to play with us. All of our equipment is in there also.

Mike also has a tub in the warming hut, and gives us warm baths. Now I never heard of huskies getting baths, but they sure feel good. The warm water soothes our aches and pains that we sometimes get from running on hard trails. When Mike finishes washing us with warm water, he then rubs us dry with a big soft towel. After he is done, we get to roll around in the straw that Mike has in the hut. Now that is a lot of fun, especially when Mike gets down in the straw and plays with us!

Lakota also told me that there are two fences between the warming hut and the building, where the trucks are parked. The two fences and the two buildings enclose our yard. Lakota said the fences are very high and keep moose and other animals out.

Lakota told me that Mike and Mary's house faces one side of the fenced yard, while the other side of the yard faces the woods. My friends Doc and Nitro led me to where everything was in the yard, and it was only a short time before I could walk around the yard without bumping into things.

As I said, I got up and was walking by the fence that faces the woods. I stopped for a second because I thought I heard

113

a sound. It was nothing, just a sound of the night. I started to walk on, but I heard it again. I strained my ears to listen. It was soft crying. I listened for a moment or two. It was not the sound of a human crying, but the crying of a dog.

"Hello." I said softly, "is anyone there?" The crying continued. "Why are you crying?" I asked. A very young voice answered, "I am scared." The voice replied. "I am lost and very hungry. I have no home and I am very cold."

"My name is Rivers," I said very gently. "Do you have a name?" I asked.

"I don't have a name." She answered. "I was born just a short time ago and given to a little girl as a gift. It was really nice for a while," she said, "but then the little girl didn't like me anymore. The big people who lived there, with the little girl, were very mean. Soon they took me to some woods and let me go. I could not find my way back to them and have been wandering in the woods for a long time." She started to cry again and begged, "Do you have some food you can give me. I am so very hungry."

"Wait here and I will get you a biscuit," I said as I rushed back to my doghouse. I got several of the biscuits Mike put in my doghouse tonight, and ran back to the fence. "Hello, are you there?" I asked, "I have some biscuits for you."

I put the biscuits on the ground and nudged them under the fence so she could get to them. As I stepped back from the fence, I heard very small footsteps slowly approach the dog biscuits. She grabbed the biscuits and started to eat them. All of a sudden, I heard her moved away from the fence very quickly. "No one is going to hurt you here. Please don't go away," I said.

"Who are you talking to, Rivers?" Lakota asked me. I told him about the little dog. He told me he did not see any dog on the other side of the fence. "Maybe you were dreaming or sleep walking," he said. "Come on Rivers. Go back to bed, it is late, and we got a big day ahead of us tomorrow."

"No" I said. "There is a little dog out there and she needs our help." Lakota started to walk away, but turned around when he heard, "Rivers, is your friend mean? No," I said. "His name is Lakota. He is a very gentle and smart dog. None of the dogs who live here are mean. We are all retired racing sled dogs."

"I am sorry I ran off Rivers, but I am so scared. I was chased by some big mean dogs the other day and…" She started to cry again. "I just don't want to remember that. I was just lucky to find hole in the wall of a shed and hid from them."

"Hi" Lakota said," I did not mean to scare you. Can you come by the fence so that we can see you?"

As I heard her walk very slowly from her hiding place, Lakota whispered to me, "Rivers, she is nothing more than a husky pup and it looks like she is hurt. She is limping." Lakota continued, "She needs our help, she can't stay out there by herself."

When she got by the fence, I heard her lay down and mumble, "I am so cold and tired."

I turned to Lakota and said, "We got to get her in to the yard. We got plenty of food and water. We can get Mike to take care of her. We…" Lakota cut me off. "Easy Rivers, I am going to get the rest of the guys. You stay here and keep talking to her."

With that, Lakota ran off to get the other dogs in the yard. Soon, the dogs were all around me. We told the little dog not to be scared. We would help her.

Nitro took charge and said. "First thing is that we have to get her into the yard. Anyone have any ideas on how to do that?"

Brownie spoke up and told us that he noticed a loose board in the back wall of the warming hut. He noticed it the last time he was in there. Ugly asked how we would get in to the warming hut. I told them that I didn't think it is locked. Maybe we could open the door. Nitro said that the doors don't close tightly and we could slip between the two front doors.

Ugly suggested that we take a couple of our harness and put them around the little dog so that we can pull here into the warming hut. "Good idea," said Doc. "Rivers, would you stay here with here and talk to her while we get to work."

Before I could answer, I heard them run off to the warming hut. I guess they squeezed through the space between the two front doors and found the loose board. Before I knew it, I heard them on the other side of the fence around our little friend.

Nitro said, "Gosh, she is so tiny, nothing more than a puppy. I can pick up her with my mouth and carry her back in the yard quicker than if we tried dragging her on these harness."

"Wake up, little one." Doc gently said, "My big friend Nitro is going to pick you, puppy style, and carry you into our yard so we help you. Okay?"

A very weak "Yes" was her reply.

Lakota told me that Nitro gently picked up the little puppy, carried her into the warming hut, and then into our yard. Several of the other dogs grab mouthfuls of straw and made a soft bed with it by our doghouses. I got all of the biscuits I had in my doghouse, while Brownie pushed over his water dish. It sounded as if it were about half full.

Lakota told me that Nitro placed the little puppy softly on the straw. I guess Doc noticed that she was shivering very badly. He told Lakota and I to curl up to the little puppy and try to keep her warm. We did this, being very careful not to roll over on her.

The shivering would not stop. I said that I think we need to get Mike. "Yes," Nitro told the guys. "Rivers is right. This puppy needs Mike. Let's all start barking and howling," I said. "That will get Mike to come out to see what is bothering us."

We all started to do that. It was not a long time before Ugly said, "Look, the back door light just went on and here comes Mike.

"Okay, okay, what is bugging you guys. What are you all doing up? Wait a minute. Where are Rivers and Lakota?"

I am not sure what happened next, but I heard Mike kneel down next to Lakota and me. "You okay?" he asked us as he started to pet us. "Well, what is this, a puppy! Where did this little one come from?" Then I guess Mike noticed the straw, biscuits, and Brownie's water dish because he said, "Don't tell me you found this puppy and are taking care of it! You boys are just amazing." He chuckled, "What a neat thing to happen at Christmas!"

I felt Mike pick up the little puppy and said, "You are in bad shape, little one. Let's get you into the warming hut and see what we can do for you."

We all followed Mike as he opened the door to the warming hut. Lakota told me that Mike turned on the lights and I heard a clicking sound. The hut started to get warmer. Mike must of saw the broken board in the back wall. "Okay" Mike said, "which one of you broke out the back board there. Let me guess," Mike continued. "Nitro, Lakota I bet it was you two since you guys are the strongest." Doc said both Lakota and Nitro's ears went down as Mike asked the question. This is a sure sign that a dog is worrying about something. Doc told me that all of the dogs' ears went down, including mine. "All of you went outside the fence?" Mike said. He must have noticed each dog with his ears down. "This puppy's neck is wet. I guess you carried her in to the yard too. Well," Mike continued, "you boys did a good thing here. Probably saved this puppy's life. You should be proud of yourselves, I know I am. Makes me very happy to know you cared enough to help another dog." You guys are just super!" I heard every single dog's tail wag when Mike said that. We knew he was not angry with us, but actually praising us for doing good.

The warming hut become nice and warm as we all sat there watching Mike check out the little puppy. "Well, she has no broken bones, but one of her rear paw pads is a little torn up. Bet she was limping a bit." Mike continued to say, "After I clean her paw, I will put some salve on it and wrap it so she doesn't lick or chew it."

I heard a whirling sound and Lakota told me that Mike put dog food into a machine and added some milk. When he turned it on, the dog food mixed with the milk to form soup. Mike put it into a bowl and gently put the puppy's face into it. "Come on little one, let's eat some of this stuff." Lakota told me the puppy was standing up and eating the food. "Good girl," Mike said, "finish it all up."

Lakota said that he got a good look at the puppy. He said that she was very dirty, but it looks like she has brown, black and white fur, and very deep blue eyes. Lakota said, "Rivers, she looks a bit like you! She has some of your markings."

Then Nitro said, "When she grows up, she will be a very beautiful dog." Nitro added. "Looks like she might also be a good racer."

Lakota asked "Nitro, how do you know she will be a good racer? She is only a puppy."

"You noticed that she has some of Rivers makings," Nitro said, "but you may not of noticed that she also has Rivers long legs and we all know that Rivers is a good racer. Believe me, Lakota, she will grow up to be a leader. Who knows," He added, "she may be a leader on our team."

I was listening to what Nitro and Lakota were saying. I told them that many dogs have my marking; they are very common. Moreover, many dogs have long legs. That does not make them good racers. I think we should be more concerned about her getting well than if she will the leader of our team one day.

After the puppy finished eating, Lakota told me that Mike wrapped her in a blanket, and placed her on a big mound of straw. Mike told us he was going back to the house to tell Mary what had happen. He would be back shortly. All of us stood by the little puppy, hoping she would be okay.

We waited very patiently for Mike to return, When he did, he started to laugh. "You boys really need to take a good look at yourselves. You are hanging around this little puppy as if she was your family. I guess she has six uncles now!"

Mike sat down on the straw next to the little puppy. We all gathered around Mike. Brownie told me that Mike was petting each one of us. When it was my turn, Mike whispered in my ear that he was very happy that I shared what I had with this pup. He said I was a true champion.

"Well, what are we going to call our little friend here?" Mike asked. A name, I thought, she does not have. "What if we call her Christmas?" he asked. "I think that is a good name, Christmas has a lot of meaning. It is a time of giving and sharing. You boys were concerned for her, got involved and gave her a chance at a new life. Now that is the true meaning of Christmas, giving and sharing."

I sat down next to the puppy, thinking about what Mike had said. I did have a gift to give to Mike after all. I made him proud of us. What more can a dog ask for than to bring joy and happiness to his human companion? Those thoughts made me feel very good. Then I heard a soft voice asking, "Rivers are you there? Yes, Christmas, I am right here." I answered.

Lakota said Christmas opened her eyes and looked at me, and said, "Thank you, Rivers for being there to hear my cry. Thank you all for saving me."

With that, Christmas closed her eyes and went to sleep. Lakota said she had a smile on her face as she slept.

Screaming Eagle

Whenever Mike gets our harnesses, we all get very excited. We know that he is going to let us run on the trails and pull our sled. I know that Mike puts the harnesses on the lead dogs first. Sometimes it is Nitro and Doc. Other times it is Doc or Nitro with one of my other buddies. Mike gives each one of us a chance to be a lead dog because Mike believes it is good for us to have that chance. Well, everyone except me. Can't have a blind lead dog, but in my dreams, I have lead our team everywhere. Sure, I wish I could see and be a lead dog. Mike tells me all the time that I would be one of the great ones, but it was not meant to be. Actually, I consider myself lucky. I have great friends, good chow, a nice bed to sleep in, and my health. I am also pain free and I have Mike.

At times, I have to remind myself of that and today was one of those days. After Mike harnessed up Doc and Lakota in lead, with the other dogs in their positions, he came to get me. I was in my doghouse and not acting as excited as my buddies were.

I heard Mike's footsteps come toward me. I heard him kneel down at the front of my doghouse. He put both of his hands on my face and gently rubbed it. He knows I like it when he does that. For so long I could not let any one near my face since my eyes always hurt so much.

In a very soft voice, Mike said to me. "You okay Rivers?" I just looked up at him and I think he got the idea that I really wanted to be left alone today. "Yep, I should of known," Mike said. "The big race is just a short time away and you know you are not going to be in it. Well as long as there is nothing physically wrong with you, you can have one day to mope. But only one and that is today." I know Mike is not happy that I am depressed. Maybe he is right and I should just let it go. Nevertheless, I really want to run it one more time before I retire.

Mike's voice woke me from my thoughts. "I'll put Sandy in your wheel position, Rivers. We will just do a short slow run just for some exercise. Mary is out also, Rivers, so it is just you and Christmas. She is in the warming shed. See ya in a while, buddy." With that, he gave me a big hug and patted my head.

I heard Mike get Sandy, who was protesting about running with the team. However, once he put her in harness, she was ready to go. Sandy started telling the guys how she was going to teach them a thing or two about trail running. We all got a good laugh out of that. Most likely, she would con her way for a free ride home in the sled basket.

Birds and dogs generally do not get along. We tend to tolerate each other and stay out of each other's way. Ravens are scavengers. Since our yard is very clean with no food or trash on the ground, they do not come by.

However, eagles do. I have heard them in the trees. I know there are two of them nesting nearby.

Eagles are strong birds and can carry off a small dog, or puppy. Eagles are very patient and will wait for their chance. With six dogs in this yard, eagles are not a problem. However, today is different. It is only Christmas and I, and Christmas is a puppy.

Mike keeps Christmas in the warming shed during our training runs. Therefore, I was not worried about her, until I heard "Hi, Uncle Rivers, whatcha doing?" I heard her paw steps at the same time I heard an eagle start to fly toward her.

Now Christmas does not know I am blind and I guess I startled her when I yelled, "Where is the eagle?" She must have seen the eagle, because I heard her running very fast toward me. At the same time, I was already running toward the sound of her paw steps, but I knew the eagle would get to her first.

I jumped at the eagle as I heard it swoop down at Christmas. My only hope was to scare the eagle and get it to fly off. While I was in the air, I told Christmas to get under my doghouse. I knew she could not get in to my doghouse since it is about a foot above ground.

As she told me she would, I felt this whack on my chest and heard a horrible screech as I fell to the ground. I was dazed, but jumped back up on my feet, and asked Christmas where she was and where the eagle was.

"Oh, Uncle Rivers, you and the big bird collided. The bird is sitting on ground between you and me. I am under the doghouse. The bird is trying to fly but one wing looks different than the other wing. Are you okay, Uncle Rivers?" I knew she was scared, but you could not tell from her voice.

"Yes Christmas," I answered, "I am fine, but I am going to walk to the doghouse and get between you and the eagle."

I heard the eagle moving on the ground. I knew the other eagle was watching and might land to be with the injured eagle.

I had to get past the injured eagle. I knew from the noise it was making, that it was on my left. I started walking around the eagle, going to my right. It started to squawk at me and I just barked back. While I was barking, I started to run to where I knew my doghouse was. I was almost there when I heard the second eagle swoop down and land.

Christmas told me the second eagle was standing by the hurt eagle and was not paying too much attention to me.

That was great. Now I had a chance to get Christmas into my doghouse and get in there also. We had to get away from these eagles and wait until Mike and the team returned.

I found Christmas, picked her up by the scruff of her neck, and put her into my doghouse. I climbed in after her and moved most of the straw to the opening to block the eagles in case they wanted to come in.

My doghouse is not too big. Mike built it so that my body heat would keep me warm in the wintertime when I slept in it. We Alaskan Huskies like to sleep outdoors and love the cold temperatures. There is plenty of fresh straw in it, which makes a nice soft bed. I always have few biscuits in there for a late night treat.

While my doghouse is a little small for two big dogs, there was plenty of room for both Christmas and me. I found one of my biscuits and gave her part of it.

I kept listening for the eagles, in case they came closer

to my doghouse. Apparently, they were staying away from us, so I knew we would be safe. I must have really hurt the one when we collided. From what Christmas said, I must have hit its wing, probably broke it. I knew the other eagle will probably stay with the hurt one, at least for a while. As soon as Mike and the team get here, the healthy eagle would fly back to the trees and watch to see what happened to its companion.

When Christmas finished her biscuit, I asked her how she got out of the warming shed. She told me that she slipped between the gap in the front doors. She was lonely and wanted to be with the team when they left. However, she was too late. Then she saw me and ran toward me. She told me she was just lonely.

"Uncle Rivers, how come you asked me where the eagle was?" Christmas asked. I told her I was blind. "You can't see!" she said very excitedly. "How did you find me that night? How did you know where the eagle was? How did you know where I was? How did you find your way back to your doghouse How...."

I cut her short and said. "Slow down with the questions, Christmas." I said. "My hearing, sense of smell and direction compensate somewhat for my lost sight. I heard you in the woods that night and I heard you run toward me in the yard just now. I heard the eagle flying toward you, and I could smell my doghouse."

"But how did you manage to collide with the eagle?" She asked.

"That was pure luck. I only hoped to jump at it and scare the bird so it would not grab you. I really did not want to collide with it. And I surely did not want to hurt it. But, well that is past." I said. "Now we sit and wait until Mike and the team gets back and makes it safe for us to go in to the yard."

After a while, I said "Mike will be upset that you got out of the warming hut, Christmas. You are too small to be in the yard by yourself with the eagles near by. It is not just the eagles you have to worry about," I said. "There are a lot of wild animals and a few mean dogs where we live. They do not normally come by our dog yard when we are all here. Some," I added, "are not very nice."

"I am sorry Uncle Rivers." Christmas said. "I just wanted to go with the team. It gets lonely when you and my other uncles are not around."

"I understand. It must be rough on you being alone when we are out. You are too small to run with the team," I said. I paused for moment thinking out loud "but I wonder if we can get Mike to let you ride in the sled basket with us."

We talked a bit more and then she fell asleep. Puppies need their rest, especially after they had an exciting day like Christmas just had. As she snored, and dreamed of being a lead dog, I listened for the eagles.

After a while, I head one fly off and then I heard Mike and the team arrive.

"Whoa," Mike said as he halted the team. "What in thunder is that in the yard! Where is Rivers?" Mike said. I heard him tie the team up, set the snow hook, and then open the gate to the yard. I stuck my head out of my doghouse. "Rivers, he said, "are you okay?" After he said that, I stuck my head back in to the doghouse, grabbed Christmas by her neck, and carried her to where Mike was standing. She woke up and Mike picked her up.

"What have you two been up to? What happened to that eagle? Look like he has a broken wing. How did you get out of the warming shed, Christmas?"

When Mike put Christmas down on the ground, I picked her up, walked through the gate to the sled, and put Christmas into the sled basket. Sandy wasn't in it.

I heard Mike walk through the gate saying "Rivers, what are you trying to tell me?"

"Come on Mike, you are a smart human. I want you to start taking Christmas with us when we run the trails. She can ride in the basket until she is big enough to run in harness with us."

I felt Mike kneel down next to me. He started to stroke my head and rub my ears, saying, "I get this feeling that something very exciting happened today in the yard. I will never know for sure, but I bet you played a big part in why there is an eagle with a broken wing in the yard, and you had Christmas in your doghouse," he said. "And now are you trying to tell me that we need to start taking Christmas with us on our trail runs? Gee Rivers, I wish you could talk."

"Yo Mike," I thought, "I wish you understood Bark."

After Mike took the hurt eagle to the vet's office for treatment, we went for a short trail run with Christmas in the basket. We all heard her giggle with happiness that she was now part of the team!

Later that night, after we returned, I was wandering around the yard thinking about what had happened today. If I had gone on the trail with the team, that eagle might have taken Christmas. I was deep in thought when I heard Lakota, Brownie and Ugly come up to me. Ugly told me that Christmas was so happy that she got to run with the team. "She kept telling us how you jumped at that eagle and save her."

"Yes," Brownie said chuckling, "she is very proud of you, Uncle Rivers."

Lakota added, "You know Rivers, you have saved Christmas two times. You are more like her guardian angel than an uncle." Then Lakota said. "You surely have a heart of gold."

"You guys are making a big thing over nothing. Each of you would do the same thing and not think twice about it. It was only a short time ago that you guys were barking at that bear to protect Missy."

"That is true, Rivers," Lakota said, "but you forget one thing. And what is that?" I asked

Lakota answered, "We see with our eyes, you see with your heart!"

As I listened to Lakota's words, all I could think about was Christmas giggling with happiness when she was on the trail with the team.

PS 49

I woke up this morning to the crunch of fresh snow under my feet after I jumped out of my dog home. How nice I thought, fresh snow always feels good on my paws. This was the soft fluffy kind. Not too wet, just right for trail running.

The other guys were sleeping in this morning, but I could feel the warmth of the sun as I wandered around our yard.

I know Mike would be getting up soon since I could smell the aroma of coffee cooking inside the big house. I tried that stuff. What a bad taste! How can Sandy drink that stuff?

Once I smelled the coffee cooking, I knew that before long we would get our morning chow.

Mike feeds us twice a day. He gives us half our daily chow in the morning and the other half at night. That way we don't feel hungry. And he snacks us with biscuits and other goodies during the day, especially if we are running the trails.

Mike adds warm water or broth to our meals so that we get plenty of water. The warm food feels so good in our tummies, especially when it is cold outside.

"Yo Rivey buddy, I see you are up bright and early this beautiful morning." It was Mike. He gave me this new nickname, Rivey, which he told me is short for Rivers. Wow, I got a name and a nickname too!

Mike got the other dogs up and started to feed us. Little Christmas was scampering around, picking up the little bits of food that we dropped or pushed out of our bowls while we were eating. The guys think this is very cute and purposely drop bits of food and biscuits for her. I know Mike feeds her very well, but puppies are always hungry.

After Christmas cleans up after all of my buddies, she comes to my food bowl and starts to push the food that I drop closer to my bowl so I can find it. Mike does this also. Soon the two of them are pushing the crumbs of biscuits, treats, and kibble back into my bowl for me to eat. It is not that I have no manners or I am a sloppy eater. When I drop food, I cannot find it, because I can not see it.

My buddies tease me about having my "personal cleaner upper." but I know that they mean no harm and they are happy to help me.

After we finished eating, Mike made sure we had plenty of fresh water. He cleaned up our yard and went back in to the big house. Lakota and I were talking about the trails when all of sudden we heard the back door open and Mike came charging out saying "Rivery, Rivery I got news for you!"

Of course we all stopped what we were doing and wondered why Mike was so excited.

I heard Mike pull up a chair and told us to gather around him. Lakota told me that Christmas jumped into Mike's lap. I sat down and heard the other dogs sit also.

Mike started talking, this was great news, and it was about the guys and me. It seems that a teacher in a far away place called New York City found my story and used that to teach her class. I turned to Doc and asked him what a teacher was. He told me that a teacher is like a musher. They teach a team or class to learn.

I understand, just like our musher teaches us to run the trails, a teacher teachers the class to …what I thought.

It was just like Mike to read my mind and answer my question. He said that humans go to school to learn many things that dogs do not need to know or know already. A teacher helps kids get ready to have a great life.

"Okay, so Mike must have had great mushers, since he is so smart" I said to Lakota. He agreed.

"So big deal" I said, "some kids like the stuff Mike wrote about me. No biggie, there have been great dogs who have accomplished great things. I just run."

Christmas must have heard me because she started to say "Uncle Rivers…" but stopped when Mike started to speak again.

I started to listen to Mike and put my thoughts on hold.

What did Mike say? These kids are special. They all have some kind of challenges in their lives. My story about being blind and running the big race twice with no sight motivated them to learn and overcome their own challenges!

Mike said that the class decorated their classroom like Alaska and made a big paper statue of me with booties on. Nitro said that Mike showed them pictures and "Rivers, the statue looks just like you!"

Then Mike started to read the letters and email that these kids sent. I listened to all of their questions and heard the guys chuckle when the kids talked about them. However, I was becoming embarrassed.

Then Mike read the mail from the kids' parents and teacher telling how I encouraged the kids to do better and learn. In addition, they wrote about the remarkable improvement in their kids' desire to learn.

I could feel the tears start to come to my eyes so I turned around and walked back to my doghouse. "Rivers," Mike called, but I needed to be alone just now. This was just too much for me, a simple country dog, to handle.

Lakota was right behind me and after I got into my doghouse he stuck his head in and asked what was the matter.

I told him I was okay. "Sure you are, Rivers. So why are you in your doghouse with tears in your eyes?"

"It shows huh" I said. "Yes my friend, it does," Lakota replied.

He knew that my tears were not of sadness, but of happiness. I was born to run and dream of crossing the finish line, helping my team and musher in the race. However, knowing about these kids, and that my story has helped them, is so much more than any dog could wish to accomplish in their life. It is very humbling to know that these wonderful kids think of me as their friend.

I heard Mike walking toward my doghouse. Lakota moved out of the opening while Mike knelt down. I knew he was looking at me. I felt his hands gently scratched my ears.

"It seems, Rivers, that your heart of gold, has touched the lives of some kids in a school very far away." Then Mike said something that really made sense to me. "Everything happens for the best. I bet that when you went blind you never would guess that your courage to overcome your challenge would help these kids." Mike continued. "It appears that your dreams of being a lead dog, squashed by your blindness, gave these kids the extra push they needed to overcome their own challenges."

Mike sure has a way to help me "see" the light with these things. As he moved away from my dog home, I got out of it and heard all of my buddies telling me how proud they were of me. Even Little Christmas told me she was very proud of her Uncle Rivers.

"Fresh snow, guys. It is trail time," Mike said. Yes, a run down a trail with fresh snow is what I need right now to help me understand all of this.

Mike started to harness us up and put us in position. I heard Christmas giggle as Mike put her in the sled basket. I was waiting for him to put me in the wheel position as usual. Instead Mike put my harness on me, snapped a neckline, and hooked me up with Lakota. Wait a minute, this is the lead dog position!

I heard Mike kneel in front of Lakota and me and gently pull both our faces to his. "You guys," Mike said, "can do this. I believe in you and know you can lead this team."

Then both Ugly and Brownie shouted, "The team does too."

You know the trail, said Nitro, "trust yourself and your instincts."

Lakota whispered to me. "I will be your eyes so you can lead us with your courage."

I heard Mike walk back to the sled basket and say his traditional "Okay team, ready, set, go!" as we started to race down the trail. Yes, I was afraid, but my confidence, the trust of my teammates, and knowing Mike believed in me overcame my fear, especially when I heard little Christmas howling with delight, "Go Uncle Rivers go!"

The Re-Start

Ⅰ heard the truck before it pulled into the driveway. I knew the sound of that truck. It belongs to Mr. Raymie. We have not seen him for a while, since he is preparing for the big race to Nome. He has his team set up and there is no need for us to go to Mr. Raymie's place to help.

Mike was in the yard with us. He had been cleaning and putting new straw into our dog homes. Christmas was running around trying to get her uncles to chase her. When they did, she ran to where Mike was and stood behind him. This generally caused her uncles to stop or run into Mike. Of course, Mike plays also by acting surprised, and then jumping back, so that he is standing behind Christmas. Brownie told me that after Mike does this, all of her uncles start to nuzzle her and she starts to giggle

Ugly, the clown, plays with Christmas a lot. Lakota told me that the last time Christmas got Ugly to chase her toward Mike, Ugly could not stop and ended up in Mike's arms. That must have looked very funny.

I guess Mike must have heard Mr. Raymie's truck in the driveway because I heard Mike walk toward the gate. Mike came past me and rubbed my ears a bit. Then I heard him walk out of the gate.

"Hi Mike, How we doing today? Mr. Raymie said.

I heard Mike answer, "Great, Raymie. I did not think we would see you before the start of the race. Bet you have been busy," Mike said.

"Well, that is what I came to talk to you about Mike, I got a problem, and I need your help."

They were walking over to the gate, so all of us started to gather by the gate to see Mr. Raymie.

"Your boys are looking good, Mike," he said. You sure take great care of them.

Thanks." Mike said. "What can I do to help you?"

"Well Mike, most of my dogs are sick, including the entire B team." They all caught some kind of bug and none of them are fit to race."

"I got five healthy dogs and that includes Rex and Smokey Joe, whom I have grave concerns about racing." he said.

"Rex is 17 years old, Raymie. How much racing can he do," he said.

Mr. Raymie said, "Mike, you know this race is very important to me. I want to borrow your team. That will give me the 12 dogs I need to start the race with." Mr. Raymie lowered his voice and said," Mike, I am not looking at wining, but just finishing this one. It is a personal thing. I need to run this race."

"Not a problem. I know my dogs would like another shot at the race, especially Rivers. Sometimes he just mopes around here. I know he does that because he knows his racing days are just about over." Mike continued, "Besides Rex and Smokey Joe, which dogs are going to race?"

Mr. Raymie answered "Fortunately, Terror, my lead dog is okay, so are Teacher, and Tarzan. Ray said that he would let his dog Junior run with me." He continued, "That gives me four very experienced dogs. I know Junior can run like the wind. That leaves one dog that is questionable, Smokey Joe."

As Mr. Raymie went on, I notice there was some excitement in his voice when he said, "Terror and Doc have run lead before and so has Nitro. Rivers, Ugly and Brownie have run this race before with me and are proven experienced runners." He added, "I know it would be a decent team that will get me to Nome."

"But what about Rex," Mike asked. "He is kind of old. You can't really expect him to go the distance."

"No I don't," answered Mr. Raymie. "I plan to use him at the ceremonial start in the city and for the restart. I will drop him at the first checkpoint. We will do a nice slow pace and I will put him in the lead position with Terror or Doc. He taught Doc and Terror to lead. They have worked well together."

Mr. Raymie continued, "I also want to use your truck, plus you and Ray will be my main dog handlers. I don't know what bug my dogs caught, but I separated the dogs that are not sick." Mr. Raymie said. "I don't know if the bug is in my truck, food or straw. I was going to ask you if I could bring the six over here until race time."

"Not a problem, but I do have concerns about Smokey Joe." Mike said. "He has had run-ins with Rex, Rivers, Teacher and Nitro."

"Yes I know," said Mr. Raymie, "but I really have no choice. The race starts in two days. I need 12 dogs to start and none of my other dogs will be well enough to run. If I don't use him, I can not run the race." Mr. Raymie added. "I will run Smokey Joe solo in the team, and drop him at the first sign of trouble."

Mike said, "Sounds like a plan, but let me give you some added insurance. All of my dogs can run lead."

Mr. Raymie replied "You must be kidding me. All of these dogs can run lead?"

Mike chuckled "Including Rivers and Lakota."

Mr. Raymie could not hide his surprise when he said. "How did you train a blind dog to lead? That is impossible!"

"It was by sheer accident," Mike answered. "I walked Rivers and Lakota together. I used a neckline and hook a leash between the two dogs. I noticed Rivers seemed to be leading the way. He was always a little bit in front of Lakota. I watched them and thought they were communicating. Both understood musher commands. I bet Lakota acts as Rivers' eyes. Add that to Rivers' sharp sense of smell, hearing, and presence, and he can compensate for his own lack of sight."

Mike went on. "When I put them in harness as lead dogs, they do okay. If you keep talking to them and do not go too fast, they can get the team to where they have to go."

"That is totally amazing!" Mr. Raymie said. "I was very worried that if Terror could not finish the race, I would be left without a lead dog. Looks like you gave me six." Mike answered, "Yes, there are six lead dogs, but two have never ran lead for you before or have they ran lead for a long trip. For this race, I would not use them as lead dogs unless there were no other choice."

Mr. Raymie replied, "I understand, Mike. It is just great to know that I have that option. You know, I bet Rivers would have been a great lead dog if he did not go blind." Mike said," Yes, he would have been. Guess we will never know."

They were quiet and I could feel them stare at me

Then Mike said "Okay Raymie, let's do it. You can use my dogs and my truck. Your team can stay here. Let's take my truck and get you dogs now. I'll let Mary know that we got company and she can get something ready for your dogs. You might as well stay for supper also. I think dessert is raspberry pie. Your favorite right?"

With that, Mike and Mr. Raymie headed toward Mike's truck in the driveway. I heard Mr. Raymie say, "Thanks Mike." After that, I heard the sounds of Mike's truck pulling out of the driveway

Wow, I am going to run the big race this year. I am so excited. I sensed that my buddies did not share my excitement. Nitro started the conversation after Mr. Raymie and Mike left

"Unbelievable," Nitro said, "it looks like us old retired racers got a chance for one more blast of glory." Doc added. "Sounds like old times don't it?" Remember the last time we ran the race together? We had some good times."

"I remember," I said, "it was a good race, we had a lot of fun."

Brownie said something that burst our bubble. "Has anyone ran with Smokey Joe?" That stopped us cold. None of even knew if he ever ran a race.

Ugly added. "He is trouble. He proved that in the yard, the last time we visited Mr. Raymie."

As we were discussing this, Lakota reminded us that Smokey Joe, as well as our other friends that we will race with, are our guests at our yard. He suggested that maybe we can change Smokey Joe's attitude by our own caring for each other. "Who knows," Lakota said, "Maybe seeing how Mike cares of us will show him that he don't have to be a bully."

"Dream on Lakota." Brownie said. "Smokey Joe bullied Rivers, picked on Rex, hissed and snarled at Mike. Remember when Smokey Joe started to make fun of Sandy?"

I remember that. I was very upset about the way Smokey Joe treated Sandy. I have never seen Sandy, but I do know she is not a husky. Mike told me she was a yellow lab, a little bit chubby, but still in good enough shape to pull a sled.

Most dogs do not care if other dogs are huskies, poodles, or sheep dogs. We were all created as equals. However, Smokey Joe started saying that because Sandy was not a husky she was inferior. Just because she did not smell like a husky she was a stupid dog.

132

I was not the only dog that got upset with Smokey Joe. Many my buddies did also. We all know that it's not right to say mean things to other dogs because they are not the same color, or their eyes are different, or they smell a little different. As Mike told us, we should be judged by what is in our hearts and not the color of our fur.

I remember I was standing next to Sandy when Smokey Joe started his nasty remarks. I was about to say something, but Sandy started talking to Smokey Joe. She asked him what he had accomplished in his life that made him think he was better than she was. "Does the color of your fur make you smarter than me?" Sandy asked. She continued, "Have you ever protected your human from danger?"

By this time, a few of my buddies came by, and started listening to what was going on. Then Doc said, "Well Smokey Joe, let's have some answers to Sandy's questions." Silence. Doc answered "But, you don't have any answers, do you? If we go by what you said, then I must remind you that blue eyed huskies are better than brown eyed huskies. But," said Doc, who has blue eyes, "any intelligent dog knows that is just bunk."

Then Sandy asked Smokey Joe, "Prove to me that you are a better dog than me just because you are a husky. Sure, you are big and tough, but that does not prove anything. I am waiting." When Smokey Joe did not answer, Sandy walked away saying, "I have no time for dealing with immature dogs who think they are better than others."

Smokey Joe started to make a move on Sandy, but Sandy heard him and said. "Yes, you really are a superior dog, got to sneak attack. You really are a disgrace to your fine husky heritage." Sandy just kept on walking away. As she did, I heard several of my buddies block Smokey Joe from going after Sandy. Teacher said, "Sure takes a big dog to go after an fine old lady like Sandy. You discredit all us, by mistreating a guest to our yard."

We were all there when this happened. I guess Lakota remembered it also since he said. "I guess all we can do is try not do anything that would cause Mike to be upset with us." We all agreed to do the best we could to be nice to Smokey Joe.

I heard the back door of the big house open, then close. "Hey guys what's up?" It was Sandy. We told her what Mike and Mr. Raymie talked about.

Trouble In The Making

We were all talking in the yard as Christmas came out of the warming shed. She liked to be around her uncles when they told stories of running races, trails, and their adventures. So she came into the group and listened very attentively. "You mean we are going to run the big race to Nome"! She exclaimed. Her outburst caught us off guard. I do not think any one realized she was in the group.

"Uncle Rivers," she said. "Are we running to Nome in the big race?" She demanded to know.

I could feel the guys look at me, waiting for me to come up with an answer that would not hurt Christmas. Yes she has been running with the team, but only as a passenger in a special basket that Mike made for her on our sled.

"Christmas," I said, "Yes we are running the big race to Nome. Unfortunately, you are too young to race with us. This was very hard, I thought "It is not our decision or Mike's." I then went on to explain why we are asked to run.

I knew she was disappointed and wanted to say something, but we heard Mike's truck pull into the driveway and the barking of our buddies from Mr. Raymie's yard.

Christmas was standing next to me and I heard Doc whisper to her, "Little One, it is not your time to shine on the trail. Take your time and don't rush to grow up."

Christmas started to speak, but Lakota cut her off. "I know our friends on that truck will treat you the way we do, but there is one bad dog named Smokey Joe, who is very mean. Do not go near him. Stay with one of us at all times when he is in the yard. He is a bully and looking for trouble."

Then Ugly, Nitro and Brownie came over to us and said we needed to go to the gate to greet our teammates and introduce Christmas. They knew about her, but had never met her.

Rex was the first one off the truck. Lakota said he looked younger than the last time we saw him. I bet knowing he will race one last time and lead our team makes him feel great inside.

Nitro welcomed Rex to the yard and introduced Christmas to him. I heard Christmas call Rex "Elder Rex" which is the ultimate sign of respect one dog can give to another, especially a younger dog to an older one. Rex replied, "Well child, thank you for the very warm welcome, but since I am related to some of your uncles, how about calling me Grandpa Rex? You may call the rest of the crew 'Uncle' also." I heard Christmas giggle and Lakota told me that Rex nuzzled her with affection.

As Mike and Mr. Raymie brought the other dogs to the yard, Christmas greeted them all with "Hi Uncle Tarzan, Hi Uncle Teacher, Hi Uncle Terror." They all made a big fuss over her.

That was, until Smokey Joe came to the yard. I heard the "Hi Uncle Smokey J...." and the gnashing and snapping of teeth, while Christmas shrieked in horror. I heard four dogs get between Smokey Joe and Christmas, but I jumped in front of all of them to confront Smokey Joe." I was very angry that he snapped at her.

"Why did you do that to Christmas?" I demanded to know. "She is just a puppy." However, Smokey Joe did not answer. Instead, I heard him move and then Nitro yell, "Look out Rivers, Smokey is going to jump you." Before I could do anything, I heard Smokey Joe yelp and fall to the ground.

I felt Christmas come to my side and heard her say she was okay, scared, but okay. Then Brownie said, "Man did you see that. Just as Smokey Joe was ready to jump Rivers, Mike grabbed him by the nape of the neck and his snout. Mike knocked Smoke Joe to the ground, and put his knee right into Smokey Joe's shoulder. Smokey Joe couldn't move, couldn't bite, and couldn't breath. You are not going to believe this," Brownie continued, "but you could see the fear in Smokey Joe's eyes." He knew he pushed to far."

"Mike," Mr. Raymie said, I need him for the race." Lakota said that he had never seen Mike so upset before. "As long as this dog stays at my yard, he wears a muzzle. Going after Christmas was totally uncalled for. Raymie," Mike said, "there is a muzzle in the shed. If you get it we can put it on him and then put him in that far corner."

Soon Mike and Mr. Raymie had Smokey Joe muzzled and located in a corner of the yard away from the rest of us.

Lakota told me that Mike brought out two chairs from the shed and set them up in the middle of the yard. Mr. Raymie asked him what he was doing. Mike said, "Every night I sit in the yard with my dogs talking to them, praising them, and giving them plenty of TLC. It seems to work because they pull harder and work better as a team." I guess they think we are all family."

We all like this community time with Mike. He is right, we are family. "So what do I do?" Mr. Raymie asked.

Mike answered, "Sit and do nothing, they will do it all." With that, I heard Rex walk over to Mr. Raymie. Lakota told me that Rex put his head onto Mr. Raymie's lap. Lakota told me that Mr. Raymie looked very surprised when Rex did that. As Mr. Raymie stroked Rex's head, I heard Rex say, "Thanks for letting me run this one last race with you. I promise to do my best and do a good job leading this team for you." Lakota told me that all of Mr. Raymie's dogs were gathering around, nuzzling him, and giving him affection.

I heard Nitro, and Brownie, then Doc, Lakota, and Ugly sit by Mr. Raymie, saying how they would race hard for him, just like in the old days. I was hesitant to do the same. Would Mike understand this simple act of loyalty for Mr. Raymie in this race? Somehow, I knew he would. I did the same. I put my head on to Mr. Raymie's lap and he rubbed my face for the first time. He hesitated at first. Mike said. "Go ahead, Raymie. His eyes are pain free and he enjoys having his face rubbed." He did and I knew that we were all committed to getting Mr. Raymie to Nome. I knew none of us would give up unless we could not go on. We felt that Mr. Raymie knew this also.

Race Day

How come race days always start so early? You would think that we would all be very excited, but we were very calm. I guess the commitment we made to Mr. Raymie last night bought us the inner peace we need to get him to Nome. We all raced with Mr. Raymie before, but none of us ever remembers him ever being this calm. Yes, we will get him to Nome.

Our bowls were full of good stuff and we all ate our fill. Christmas was scampering around playing with us, wishing us good luck, and still begging us to take her with us. She did not go near Smokey Joe, who was eating and snarling at the same time.

Sandy was in the yard also. She was not there to "clean our houses" like she normally does, but to wish us good luck. We were all surprised when she started talking to Terror, Rex and Doc, who were discussing lead dog strategies. "Now you two better take good care of my boys or else I will give you a good piece of my mind when you get back. You understand?" All we heard was Rex and Terror say "Yes ma'am we will do out best. "Well," Sandy said, "that is all I wanted to hear. You have a great race and good luck to you. And Rex, do not go showing up the kids too much. You know how they get bruised pride when we old folks do them in!"

Rex started to laugh. "Yes I will remember that."

Then Sandy came over to Lakota and me and said, "I got this feeling you guys are starting on a great adventure. I just wanted to let you know that I am proud of you. Have a great race and especially a safe one. Lakota, don't forget that you have to reign Rivers in. Sometimes his courage and heart overload his common sense." Lakota said he would do his best.

Then Sandy said to me. "Be careful of Smokey Joe, Rivers. I heard what happened last night. He will save his cheap shots for the trail. Mr. Raymie may not be wise to him like Mike is. Mr. Raymie will be concentrating on the race and may not be there when Smokey Joe acts up. Remember, Rivers, your job is to get this team to Nome and not to settle scores with Smokey Joe. There is an old saying, 'what goes around comes around.' Believe me, Smokey Joe will get his just rewards."

"Now where is that Christmas?" Sandy said. "Come on, child, I will show you how to clean doghouse after these bozos leave to run all over the country side."

"Aunt Sandy, my uncles and Grandpa are running the big race to Nome, not running all over the country side." Christmas said. "Whatever, child," Sandy said, "come with me so we can start cleaning these doghouses. Let's start with the shed." Sandy sighed.

"Uncle Rivers, please take me with you." Christmas pleaded. "I don't want to clean doghouses. I want to be a racing sled dog like you." Lakota and I started to laugh, and told Christmas that Aunt Sandy cleans the treats out of our dog houses. That is what she means by cleaning dog houses. "Oh, well in that case," she said, "I'm coming, Aunt Sandy."

After we had finished eating and relaxed a bit, Mike came out of the big house and started to load us into the big dog box on his truck. There was a problem. It seems that Mike's dog box is not big enough to hold all of us dogs, especially since Smokey Joe can not be put into a box with another dog. We can't leave any dogs. I was wondering about that when Mike picked me up. He put me in the front seat of his truck with a harness on me to hold me in. All right co-leader time, I thought. What surprised me even more was when he put Doc and Lakota in the back seat of the truck. "All set?" Mike said. "We got all the dogs in the truck and we will met Raymie at the starting point. He is bringing the sled and gear plus harnesses he needs for the race."

After what seemed a short trip, we were in the city. We met

Mr. Raymie. Mike told Mr. Raymie that he would put us in harness, while Mr. Raymie got the sled and gear together. Mr. Raymie told Mike our positions in the team. Lakota and I would be in the wheel. Brownie and Nitro would run in front of us. Smokey Joe would be running alone. In front of him would be Ugly and Teacher. Next would come Junior and Tarzan behind Terror and Doc. Rex would run solo lead.

I was getting excited. There were a lot of people cheering. I heard the click of camera and the other dogs on the other teams. Many were old friends. I remember the last time I raced. I felt so good.

I felt Mike put my harness on and gave me one of his great body rubs. I was ready.

"Hey runt!" It was Smokey Joe. "You better watch your tail, I going to get it on this trail and get even with you for what Mike did to me last night."

"No you are not." It was Nitro. "You better look who is running behind you."

And then Teacher said, "Look who is running in front of you, me!"

Then Lakota said. "I am right here for Rivers also." Every dog in the team gave a warning to Smokey Joe that he had better not try anything stupid.

"Then I will just bite Mike when he puts the harness on me." Smokey Joe said. "That will stop this show but good."

Rex had enough. He said, "You are not going to bite anyone for two reasons. First, if you bite someone in this city, they put you in the dog pound. There is no coming back from the pound. A friend of mine is available to race in your place. Second reason is that you still got that muzzle on. So how are you going to bite anyone with a muzzle on? Stop being so immature and start living up to your husky heritage."

Sometimes you have to wonder if Smokey Joe has all paws on the ground.

I turned to Lakota and asked him if Mr. Raymie had his racing bib on yet. Lakota told me he did and we are the number three team to leave. That means we go in about six minutes.

I heard Mike finish putting the harnesses on the dogs, giving each one good hug.

Yes we are ready.

Rex said "here is the plan. We got fresh snow and a fast trail to the first checkpoint. After that we go back to Mr. Mike's and then do the restart tomorrow. So we are going to take a nice easy run in the city. No need to race to the first checkpoint." Let's use this run to tuneup our teamwork.

Yes, a great plan. Let's go.

I heard Mr. Raymie get on the sled runners. A voice yelled. "Number three team into the chute." That's us!

Mike and Mr. Raymie were taking and laughing about something. They are sure relaxed I thought.

"Ten, nine, eight (it is our time) seven, six, five, four (I start to pull against my harness) three, two, one, Go!" And, we are off. As we run down Race Street to the trail, I heard Christmas giggling as she yells, "Go, Uncle Rivers, go! Go, team, go!"

Starting Down The Trail

Wow, this was great! There was fresh snow on the trail. Rex was keeping a nice even pace and the team was enjoying the run. Mr. Raymie's commands of "Gee" (right) and "Haw" (left) were crisp. Even the weather was near perfect for mushing. The crowds cheering us on at the beginning were thinning out. Occasionally a would person yell "Good luck" or "Have a safe run."

Soon we had the trail to ourselves. Sure, there were teams running before us and after us, but we had this little envelope of peace and tranquility. Rex knew the way, so Mr. Raymie did not have to give too many commands. The guys seem to be enjoying themselves. Ugly and Lakota were telling jokes. Normally, Ugly is the jokester, but lately Lakota has been telling some real good ones.

I heard Terror and Doc say how good Rex looked. They were teasing him that he was making us look bad. Imagine Rex, a 17-year-old veteran, running with the energy and enthusiasm of a three-year-old. Impressive! I hope he can make it all the way to Nome. That would be remarkable.

It seemed that all the guys were enjoying themselves, except for Smokey Joe. No sooner than we were alone on the trail, he started complaining about everything. The snow was too soft. The pace is too slow. Mr. Raymie didn't speak loud enough. His harness was too tight. When were we going to get there? When did we eat?

I know I wanted to tell him to be quiet and probably most of the other guys wanted to do the same, but we just ignored him. However, Rex had enough and told Smokey Joe to stop whining and start living up to his husky heritage.

Smokey Joe told Rex that he isn't taking orders from some old has-been. Nitro, who was directly behind Smokey Joe, told him he had no respect for his elders. Lakota, running next to me, said that Smokey Joe turned around to snarl at Nitro and stumbled, into Junior. Mr. Raymie halted the team to prevent Smokey Joe from being run over by the sled.

Smokey Joe immediately started to blame Junior, but Junior stopped Smokey Joe cold. Junior said. "Before you go shoot off your jaw, Smokey Joe, keep in mind that Tarzan and I are brothers and Spot is our dad. You gave our dad a bad time in Mr. Raymie's yard. Remember?"

Then Tarzan added, in a very menacing voice "So we are watching you."

Smokey Joe just grumbled. Rex said, "Smokey Joe, you are not making any friends on this team and believe me, with out team support, you will not make it to Nome.

"Who said I was going to Nome," Smokey Joe said. "I got my excuse to get off this team and go back to the yard, lay in my coop, eat hot chow and enjoy the leisurely life, while you jokers work your tails off getting some human to Nome."

"And," Smokey Joe said, "if you trail bunnies keep messing with me, I will spoil this trip for all of you. Just stay out of my way and I will get off this team very soon."

Now we knew the score. Smokey Joe was either going to get off this team before we got to Nome or do something to get us pulled from the race

I know Nitro and Teacher were very upset with this, but they kept quiet. What could we say? "Let's make a deal Smokey Joe." Doc said, "Tomorrow is the restart. It will be as hectic as today, what with people running around getting things done. No one will pay any attention to you. However," Doc said, "the first check point is only 20 miles after the restart. That would be the best place for you to get off the team. It is a short hop back to Mr. Raymie's yard and you won't have to stay overnight at the checkpoint waiting for a ride. I am sure the team will work with you if you will work with us through the restart. Deal?"

"Deal" Smokey Joe said, "but just one more thing. I want some extra treats. I have not been getting any lately."

I knew the guys would be really upset. So I said. "You seem

to have a bone to pick with me and Mike. These guys have nothing to do with that. I will give you all of the treats in my coop if you agree to Doc's plan. After the next checkpoint, we will be going back to Mike's place until the restart tomorrow."

"You know, runt," Smokey Joe said, "getting all of your treats just makes this deal a lot sweeter."

Lakota said to me very softly "Rivers, it is not right for you to give up all of your treats to get Smokey Joe to work with us."

I replied. "It is not right, but if he stays on this team, there will be trouble and he can stop us from getting Mr. Raymie to Nome. We don't need him except to ensure that we have 12 dogs for the restart. After that, it don't matter. Besides, has he been pulling his weight? I bet his line has been slack for this entire run. Teacher and Nitro are pulling his share of the load."

Lakota said, "I know you are right, but it is so wrong to give into him. There must...."

I interrupted Lakota. "We all committed to helping Mr. Raymie get to Nome, but Smokey Joe didn't. He has no honor or shame. He just don't care. We will do better without him. Giving up my treats to get him off this team is well worth it."

Lakota had no answer. I knew he disapproved, but I bet he knew I was right.

Nitro must have overhead me. He said. "I want to be there when you give him your treats. I want to make sure he don't try to jump you."

"Yeah, I want to go too," Lakota said.

Then Brownie said the same, adding, "I will make sure all of the guys know. We will be there for you, Rivers." Brownie said, "And I will give you some of my treats to replace some of the ones you are giving Smokey Joe."

Me too," said Ugly, Nitro and Lakota.

It made me feel good to know that I had friends like this.

We were starting to climb the last hill before we entered the first checkpoint. The team was running well, but I heard paw steps that were out of sync with the rest of the team. Lakota said. "He is starting his act, Smoky Joe has a slight limp."

We entered the checkpoint and I heard Mr. Raymie drop the snow hook. He started to walk over to Smokey Joe. Lakota told me that Mr. Raymie was checking out Smokey Joe's leg. Then I heard Mike ask Raymie what he was doing.

"Smokey Joe took a tumble a bit back on the trail and started to limp slightly on the last hill. It is a very slight limp. I will take a good look at him at your place. I am sure he will be okay, but I will keep an eye on him after the restart tomorrow."

They discussed the run as they got us out of harness and packed away the gear. Mr. Raymie was very pleased and said we did very well on trail.

After we got back to Mike place and were given some great hot chow, we had our community time. After Mike and Mr. Raymie left, Smokey asked me where his treats were.

"I am bringing them." I said. As I got them out of my coop, Lakota, Nitro and Brownie, and all of the other dogs were right there to help. My buddies helped me carry the treats to Smokey Joe.

"Yes" he said, "Tribute to the king."

I heard Nitro start to say something, but Doc told Nitro it was not worth it.

Doc said. "okay Smokey Joe, here is the plan. Mr. Raymie noticed your slight limp today. After we start down the trail tomorrow, and we get past the crowd, start limping a lot and maybe even howl in pain. Mr. Raymie will stop the team to check you out. He will think that you can't walk on your paw and put you in the basket for the run to the next checkpoint. At that checkpoint, he will turn you over to a vet, who will make sure you get back to the yard."

"Good plan Doc, I could not think of a better one myself." Smokey Joe said. "Say runt, these treats are very good." Smokey Joe said to me.

Doc spoke before I could. "We kept our end of the deal, will you keep yours?"

Smokey Joe said, "Why not, I get out of the race, and still get to keep all of these treats."

We all walked back to our coops. I was chuckling very softly and Doc asked me why I was chuckling. Lakota asked also. I told them that the treats I gave Smokey Joe were spoiled and he will get a good tummy ache on the trail tomorrow. Mr. Raymie will have no choice, but to drop Smokey Joe at the checkpoint.

Lakota asked how I knew the treats were bad. I answered, "Because Sandy never took them. She told me that they were very, very old and spoiled. She warned me that if I ate them I would get sick. I just never got rid of them."

"You mean…." Lakota said.

But I interrupted him. "That's right, about a mile down the trail tomorrow, Smokey Joe is going to be one sick puppy."

"Rivers, you are one clever doggie." Doc said. "Yes," Lakota added, "Clever and sly."

"No," I said, "I am committed to getting Mr. Raymie to Nome and Smokey Joe can't be trusted. So we got some insurance that he will be dropped after the restart tomorrow."

Later that night, we all gathered round to talk and tell stories. We invited Smokey Joe to join us and he did. Rex was telling us a story about one of his races, when the quiet of the night was broken by the piercing howl of a wolf.

"What's that?" Smokey Joe said.

"It is a wolf howling" Ugly said.

Smokey Joe asked what a wolf was. Doc told him that wolves and dogs are related. Some humans believe that dogs, especially huskies are the direct descendents of wolves.

"Maybe that is why I am so superior to you guys, I am really a wolf." Smokey Joe said. No one answered. We were just fascinated at how Smokey Joe could picture that. He went on and on about how strong he was, and how smart he was. Of course, he had to mention how tough he was also. We just let him talk and talk. Soon we got very tired and one by one, we drifted off to our coops. I understand he stayed up most the night convincing himself he was a wolf.

Restarting Again

The restart was a repeat of the ceremonial start in the city except that there were fewer people and we started on an actual trail and not on a city street. The weather was perfect for mushing. We had new snow and I was feeling very good, until Mike put this huge body hug on me and told me he would see me when I get back from Nome. I forgot about that. Mike is not going to be on the trail with us. I was starting to feel sad. Mike said. "I know you want to run this race, Rivers, and I want you to have it. I can't come with you. You don't need me to do it with you. Do your best and cross that finish line knowing that you are a true champion."

Mike said good words and gave body hugs to each of us. I know we all wanted him to be with us, but he could not. He is right. This race is for us. This race is for Mr. Raymie. It is not for the glory; it is for the accomplishment.

On cue, Smokey Joe started to limp, but before Mr. Raymie could stop the team and get to him, he got real sick. I mean very sick. Lakota told me that he never saw a dog get so messy while he was sick. Whatever Smokey Joe ate yesterday and this morning, was sure coming out now. We lost a lot of time getting to the checkpoint and dropping Smokey Joe off. Once we did, the entire team's attitude changed for the better. We were running as one, with a purpose, and a can-do attitude!

The trail turned horrible. There was very little snow. We crossed open water where there should have been ice. The temperatures were warm, even at night. We passed several other teams that had broken sleds caused by traveling over the

146

rocky trail. At each checkpoint, we heard that many dogs were dropped, due to sore paws from walking on the terrible trail.

We also heard of many sick dogs that caught the same bug that crippled Mr. Raymie's team. We all thought it must be the warm weather causing it. We considered ourselves lucky. While none us of had sore paws, we had our share of sore muscles. While we were hurting, we were not going to give up. Not even Elder Rex. Between his skill as a lead dog, and Mr. Raymie's experience as a musher, we avoided a lot of the stuff that hurt the other teams.

We did not stay in the checkpoints like the other teams. Mr. Raymie checked in and then out of the checkpoint very quickly. We would camp out several miles down the trail. Mr. Raymie said that this way we would get more rest, since there would not be any other teams around us.

Mr. Raymie would lay down fresh straw for us. Then he would check out our paws and change out booties. With the absence of snow, we were wearing our booties for most of the trip. After we were all settled in, Mr. Raymie would either gives us a snack (he makes the best fishicles) or a hot meal, depending if we were staying at the camp for a long time. He made sure we had plenty of warm water. As we were chowing down and relaxing, Mr. Raymie would make himself something to eat. When he was finished, Mr. Raymie would check us over again, give us some ear rubs, and tell us he was proud of us for doing a good job. Wow, a full belly, fresh straw, some ear rubs, and some good words. What more can you ask for?

I guess I heard the sled first and then my buddies heard it also. It stopped near us. I heard Mr. Raymie say to the other team, "How we doing, Musher John? Your team looks very good. I see they got you through the bad trail okay. No damage to your sled?"

"Musher Raymie," Mr. John said, "Good to see you. I missed you at the start and restart. Looks like your team is doing well also. Down to 11 dogs I see."

"Well, I started with 12. That bug hit my yard and…"

Mr. John interrupted Mr. Raymie. "Wait a minute. Is that Rivers and Lakota? And Terror, is that you? Why, is that Old Rex?"

I know Mr. John. Lakota, Terror, and I came from his yard. He gave us to Mr. Raymie.

147

I heard Mr. John walk toward me. I knew he was very close. I surprised him by holding up my paw to shake. Mike says that humans like to shake our paws as a sign of greeting.

Mr. John shook my paw and said, "Rivers, you are looking well. I see your eyes are better. "I heard about your buddy, Mike, and what he did for you."

I heard Lakota raise his paw also. "Why shy Lakota, you don't seem so shy now. What happen to you?"

Mr. Raymie said. "Rivers and Lakota live with Mike. So do Doc, Ugly, Nitro and Brownie. Mike let me borrow his team when he found out that all of my dogs got sick. That is the reason why I am using Rex as my lead dog."

"You are using Rex as your lead dog!" Mr. John said. "Why he must be 14 years old!" How is he doing?"

Mr. Raymie replied, "Rex is 17 and I have been very surprised by him. He runs like he did 10 years ago. He helped me avoid a lot of the trouble on the trail back there."

Mr. John said. "Let me take care of my team, and then we can share a campfire. Okay?"

"Sure," Mr. Raymie said. "You know I enjoy your company."

Later, after Mr. John took care of his team, he came over to our team and sat down with Mr. Raymie. "I can't stay too long, Musher Raymie. You know this is a race and I think my team has a great chance. "

Mr. Raymie said. "You have a great looking team, Musher John. I hope you win it. My guys here are making a great showing. Don't know how we will do, but we will finish."

"By the way, Musher Raymie, didn't you drop a dog named Smokey Joe a while back?"

"Sure did. Started limping and tossed his cookies from both ends. Never seen a dog get that sick so quickly. All the dogs ate the same stuff for the last two days. Guess he got into something I did not know about."

All the guys started to laugh and mumble something about "Rivers' special treats!"

"Well," said Mr. John, "Your dog got away from the dog handler trying to get him ready for the trip back to your yard. From what I heard, he actually tried to bite the handler who lost his grip on your dog's collar. Last they saw of him, he was heading in the direction of that wolf pack that lives near that checkpoint."

Doc said. "Well I'll be, Smokey Joe joining a wolf pack. Wonder how long that will last."

Mr. Raymie said. "He was a trouble dog. I bet that he won't last too long with any wolf pack. As soon as he starts his trouble, they will get rid of him. Some dogs just have to learn the hard way."

"Well," Mr. John said," I got to get going. Good luck to you and your team. Hey Rivers, Lakota and Terror, remember to stop in Nome. I don't think Musher Raymie wants to go to my yard in Kotzebue!" I could hear Mr. John laughing as he got his team lined up and took off down the trail.

Mr. Raymie was laughing also. "Good man that Musher John. I hope he does win this race. Well team, it nap time."

It was sure great to meet Mr. John again. Both Terror and Lakota told me that Mr. John's team looked very good. All the dogs looked like Terror, Lakota, or me, only younger. Nitro broke our chain of thought when he said. "Mr. John's dogs were very respectful of you three. Do you know them." We answered "no, we didn't," but that is one of the trademarks of Mr. John's dogs. They are very friendly, very respectful, and very loyal to their musher. However, most importantly, they all have a great desire to run.

When we woke up, we had snow on the ground. Fresh snow would make the trail easier to run.

When Mr., Raymie told us to line up, we all did, except for Elder Rex. He did not get up.

Terror was behind Rex saying "Rex, Rex, you okay?"

"Yes, I am okay, but I can't go on. This old body just can't keep up with my young spirit. I have done my part. It is up to you guys to get Mr. Raymie to Nome."

"We will take you with us, in the basket," Teacher said. "No!" Rex replied, "You don't need to carry the extra weight. My spirit will be with you on the trail. You can tell me all about it when you get back from Nome."

I heard Mr. Raymie walk up to Elder Rex and say, "Can't go on, Rex? You took me farther than I ever thought you could. Here, let me pick you up and put you in the basket." We will get you back to Mike's place, and you can wait for me there. Thank you, my friend, for doing your part and getting me this far on the trail."

We all were very sad. We wanted Elder Rex to lead us to Nome. As we raced down the trail to our next checkpoint, Elder Rex kept giving us encouragement. As we dropped him off, he turned around and said to all of us. "Thank you for following me down this trail. Please take good care of my musher, and get him to Nome." We all told Rex not to worry; we would do our best. I could not see Elder Rex, but I knew he was watching us leave the checkpoint. I knew he wanted to come, I felt his spirit with us. Terror and Doc were the lead dogs now. I know they would not let Elder Rex down.

After we said good-bye to Elder Rex, Terror and Doc led the team down the trail. The fresh snow made the going easier, and we were making some very good time. Ugly and Lakota continued to swap jokes. Nitro was in the wheel position with me. Nitro likes to tell me about what he sees on the trails. Like Lakota, he acts like my eyes at times. All of these guys are just great.

We were racing at night. The only sounds we heard were the wind in our fur, and the sled runners dancing on the snow. We were all lost in our own thoughts. It was very peaceful.

The checkpoints came very quickly now. I guess because the trail was so much better than at the beginning of the race. After awhile, I knew there was only one more checkpoint left before Nome. Soon Nitro told me we were entering the last check point. It seemed like a short run before I heard the laughter of children, and then Mr. Raymie saying "Whoa," telling us to stop. I knew the local children were all around us, petting us and making a big fuss over us. I like it when the kids do this and talk to us. Since my operation, I am not afraid of the kids touching my face or rubbing my ears. Nitro kept telling me when the kids were near me, so I would not be startled when they petted me. The kids don't know I am blind.

I head Mr. Raymie talking to the check-in official. They were discussing the weather, and the possibility of a bad storm hitting the coast. There was always that possibility. The coast is noted for having unpredictable bad storms. We all have heard horror stories of teams getting caught in a bad storm, losing direction, and actually heading out to sea on the sea ice, never to be seen or heard from again.

We took a short break, and Mr. Raymie checked us all over. We had 10 dogs, where most teams had seven or eight. For a bunch of retired old dogs, we were in good shape and well rested. The young dogs on the team were doing fine also. They are a good bunch and I know Mr. Raymie is very proud of them.

Mr. Raymie told the official that he was heading out and felt he could out run the storm, if it did hit the coast. Before we left, he gave us each a fishicles and put fresh booties on our paws. Mr. Raymie changed out positions too. He had Terror and Doc in lead, with Nitro and Teacher in swing. Tarzan and Junior were next with Brownie and Ugly behind them. Lakota and I were in wheel. This was a smart move on Mr. Raymie's part. He had three lead dogs in front with Terror, Doc, and Nitro. Those three have run together the longest, so he has his most experience leaders in front.

I was ready to go, when I heard Mr. Raymie open the sled bag. After he got something out of it, he zipped the bag closed and walked over to the team. Lakota told me that Mr. Raymie had something in his hand that it smelled terrific. Yes, I smelled it also. "Mike made me promise that when we got to the last checkpoint I give each of you dogs one of these very special treats," Mr. Raymie said as he put the treat in front of my nose. Wow, these are great! Mike and Mary make them special for us. We only get them on special occasions.

I heard Ugly say, "Mike let us run this race for ourselves and to help Mr. Raymie get to Nome. Let's run the last leg of this race for Mike!" We all agreed to run the best we could in this final part of the race. We won't win, but we are sure going to make Mike proud of us.

We set out on the trail, determined to run it as fast as we could. The trail was smooth and fast. We were making great time. But, the temperature was dropping very fast, and I could smell the scent of a storm. Nome and the finish of the race were just down the trail, but first we had to cross the frozen Norton Sound. If a storm caught us while crossing the Sound, the going would get really tough and dangerous.

We were traveling very fast, but the storm scent was getting stronger. I knew we would not outrun it at our current speed.

I mentioned this to Terror and Doc, and they suggested we pick up the pace a little and try to out distance the storm. Getting closer to the shore was the idea.

Mr. Raymie slowed us down because he did not know the storm was coming in. I bet he was afraid to "burn us out" by going too fast. I remember the race official telling Mr. Raymie that there might be a storm approaching. In addition, we all knew that Mr. Raymie was very, very tired. Mushers don't get much sleep during the race, and I bet Mr. Raymie dozed off on the sled runners a few times, while we were on the trail. That is the point of having great lead dogs. They always know where they are going.

I knew this storm would catch us. Many teams have lost their sense of direction in bad storms, and well I don't want to think about that. I concentrated on listening for cracking sea ice. That is a good sign that we may be going the wrong direction, out to sea. Mr. Raymie would not hear that, especially with the wind was howling in his ears.

There was no warning when the storm hit us. One minute it was clear and cold, the next the storm was beating us with swirling, blowing snow. The wind came from all directions. The roar of the wind was awful. The guys said they could not see any trail markers. The snow was falling very fast, making the trail, or what we thought was the trail, hard to run on.

We slowed our pace. The leaders could not find the way. We were getting lost.

I heard it. A slight cracking sound. I knew the leaders or Mr. Raymie would not hear it. Then I smelled the salt. Sea ice! We were heading in the wrong direction!

"Terror, Doc, Nitro, We are heading in the wrong direction," I said, "I heard ice cracking and smell salt."

"Are you sure?" Terror said, "I can't hear, see or smell anything. These conditions are the worse I have ever been in. Maybe we need to stop."

"No, no, we can't stop," Brownie yelled. "We could be so close to the sea that we may end up on an ice flow. No we must keep on going."

"But in which direction?" Doc said," I can't see or hear anything either. How about you Nitro, can you find our way?

"I am like you, I don't know which way to go."

"Rivers does." It was Lakota. I was surprised. What is he up to I thought. "You can't see. Rivers can't see either. But he hears and smells things better than we do. I know he can lead us out of this."

"Lakota is right" It was Doc. "Rivers has run lead with Lakota, and we have never had a problem. "I think we need to have him up front to guide us out of this mess."

"Yeah, I am for that." It was Ugly. "Let's get Rivers into lead with Lakota."

"But how are we going to do that," Brownie said.

"We just stop running and when Mr. Raymie gets off the sled to find out why we stopped, we all gather around Rivers and Lakota." Terror answered.

"Yes, that would work," Nitro said. "We can actually get behind Rivers and Lakota and show Mr. Raymie what we want to do."

So they did. We all stopped. Mr. Raymie got off the sled. I heard the snow anchor jammed into the snow. "This is one bad storm, Terror you having.... What are you dogs doing moving behind Lakota and Rivers like that?"

I bet Mr. Raymie remember Mike's words the night before we left about lead dogs. "I am giving you six lead dogs, all can run lead, including Rivers and Lakota."

"I am lost and so are my lead dogs who have stopped running because they can't find the trail," Mr. Raymie said to no one in particular. At that moment, the wind changed directions and we all got a good whiff of salty air and then the cracking sound. It was loud and shook the ice under us.

"Jeez!" Mr. Raymie said. "Okay Rivers and Lakota. Mike said you could do this so get us out of here and back to shore." He repositioned us. Lakota and I were in lead, Nitro and Doc in swing, Terror and Teacher came behind them, with Tarzan and Junior following them. Ugly and Brownie were in the wheel.

I heard another crack, and decided to waste no time. I headed in a direction away from the sound I heard. I guess in my haste, I forgot about the snow hook and Mr. Raymie. Ugly started to laugh, saying that I ripped the snow hook out of the ground, and Mr. Raymie barely got on the sled runners in time.

The brakes were off and we were running at top speed. I felt that our time was running out. We were very close to the sea. Our only chance was to run in the opposite direction from the sounds I heard.

I heard another crack, but it was little fainter. It was starting to become a wild run. Nitro was directly behind me. He said he could hardly see my ears, because the snow was blowing so hard. Lakota kept telling me what he could see in front of us. He said there was nothing but blowing snow.

We were running very, very fast. Even the speedsters, Junior and Tarzan joked that they did not know us old geezers could run this fast. Yeah, funny how fear can make you run like the wind. I knew they joked to hide their own fears.

A thunderous roar to our front, sharp turn to the right, more speed. We were further out then we had thought we were! We were zigzagging to avoid the cracking sounds I heard. Another crack, but a little fainter now. The wind was picking up. It was to our backs, and was loaded with salt smells. We must be running away from the sea.

Soon I felt the slight incline, as we continued to run as fast as we could. I knew we were close to the land and safety. The ice would be thicker now. The chances of it breaking off and floating out to sea were very small. I let up on the speed, and told the team we were safe.

We found the trail again and Mr. Raymie stopped the team. "Good boy, Rivers. Good boy, Lakota. Good team." He heaped a lot of praise on us. I knew he would put Terror and Doc back in to lead. It was only fair, they are the lead dogs and did a great job. It wasn't their fault we became lost. Things like that happen.

Mr. Raymie started to put Terror back in lead. Lakota told me that Terror just sat down. Then Doc and Nitro also sat down. Lakota then told me that the entire team sat down and he and I were the only dogs standing.

"Terror, what are you doing?" I asked. "Rivers, I have been a lead dog for a long time and have lead teams across the finish line in Nome. You deserve this finish."

"Yeah, Rivers." It was Nitro." You saved our tails. Now lead us to the finish!" I was barkless.

"Well Rivers and Lakota, looks like you are my lead dogs

154

for the last few miles to Nome." Mr. Raymie said. "Okay, line up." Lakota told me that all the dogs stood up and looked sharp. "Hike, hike" and we were off.

The last few miles were a joy to run. The storm had calmed down. Mr. Raymie was giving mushing commands and Lakota was telling me what we were passing on the trail.

I heard the siren and then people cheering us on. Lakota told me we were almost at the finishing line. He described the finishing chute and just as he said that we crossed the finish line, I heard, "Way to go, Uncle Rivers, lead dog!" It was Christmas and that meant Mike was here also! As I stopped the team, I felt familiar hands giving me a big body hug.

After Thoughts

The race is over and we did our part. We got Mr. Raymie to Nome. While he stayed for the mushers banquet, Mike took the entire team back home by airplane shortly after we crossed the finish line.

I was glad he did. I can image the fuss that would happen if people knew I was blind and the lead dog. Rivers, a lead dog! I still cannot believe that I was a lead dog. Sure, I dreamed about it, but never knew if I could make the grade. I guess I did.

I am not sure what position we came in. I know we were not last. I heard people remark about how old we were compared to the other teams. Other people remarked about how good we looked, and how fast we were for an older team. I am glad we crossed the finish line at night. No one could see that a blind dog was leading this team. Actually, I did have my eyes with me. Nine pairs all looking out for me and helping me lead the way.

I am not much for flying, and spent most of the flight thinking about what happened after we crossed the finish line.

Once we reached Nome, Mike and Christmas met us. Mike put Christmas in the sled basket and took the team to the rest area. Mr. Raymie talked to the race officials and did his musher chores.

On the trail to the rest area, we all chuckled at Christmas and her nonstop questions about what happen on the trail, where is Smokey Joe and on and on. She told us that Elder Rex was resting and doing very well at our yard. We were all relieved when we heard that Elder Rex was okay. Christmas also mentioned that Aunt Sandy was worried about us, but Sandy will never admit it. You would never think that she had a heart of gold, but she does…. Remember that she would not even talk to me when we first met, and now she worries about the guys and me while we were on the trail.

Mike took us out of harness, and led us to some fresh straw. As we relaxed, he gave us some warm chow and checked over our paws. He put soothing salve on them. We all were lucky, no paw problems, but it is always nice to get a foot massage with stuff to make our paws feel better.

Mike was not saying much, but Lakota kept telling me that every time he passed me, he just shook his head and had a big grin on his face.

"Wow Rivers, he is sure proud of you." Lakota said.

"Nah," I said. "Knowing Mike, he is proud of all of us."

"Yep," said Nitro. "There is a lot of affection in those ear rubs he has been passing out since we got out of our harness."

I was getting tired. I guess the excitement of this entire adventure really started to hit me. The last thing I remember before I went to sleep on the airplane was Lakota, joking with Ugly. "Did you hear the one about the poodle?"

Back Home

Yes I love to run the trails, but I like it better when I get home. After this adventure, home was just great. There was fresh straw in our doghouses and fresh treats stashed in each one. I was getting cozy in my doghouse when Elder Rex, came by and asked if he could talk to me.

"Sure Elder Rex. It is always a privilege to have you talk to me." I replied.

"No son, the honor is mine." He said. "Terror told me what you did on the trail. You saved your musher and your team. The ultimate that a lead dog can do. You made me proud to be your leader for the short time I ran with you. You are a credit to our husky tradition."

I was barkless. These words were coming from a veteran lead dog; a great lead dog; a lead dog I would follow on any trail, no matter how old he was. As I said, I was barkless.

Elder Rex continued, "We are returning to our yard tomorrow. I want you to know that it has been a great pleasure staying here with your team and sharing the trail with you. The next time we run a trail, I hope we can run lead together."

"That would be my pleasure also, Elder Rex." I replied humbly.

"Good night, Rivers." Elder Rex said as he went back to his doghouse.

After awhile, I head Mike come into the yard. He gave treats to all of the dogs. When he was done and he gave me my treat, Mike clipped a leash on me. We were going for a walk! I may have just returned from racing a long race, but I always have energy for a nice walk.

Yes, I love to walk with Mike. We started down the trail we normally run. There was a light dusting of fresh snow and Mike was describing the night sky, and the full moon. Funny, whenever Mike describes these things to me, it is as if I can see them with my own eyes.

"Rivers, let's sit down on this old log over here." Mike said. We sat down. I was sitting with my back to him. He was stroking my head. Then all of a sudden, he puts this huge body hug on me.

"You amaze me," Mike continued. "You, a blind dog, leading your team to safety through a blinding blizzard. They say that storm was one of the worst fast moving storms that has hit the Coast in years. Simply amazing! Mr. Raymie told me that when Terror and Doc got lost on the sea ice, he thought you all were goners."

I did not know that, I thought to myself, while Mike continued. "Mr. Raymie said he just let you go in whatever direction you thought best. He had no idea which direction to go. However, Mr. Raymie did say you seemed to know."

I had no idea which direction we were going in, all I did was lead the team away from the cracking sound and put the salt smell to our backs.

"I knew you were a true champion, and now you proved it to everyone." Here; I have something for you," Mike continued.

"It is a shame that there are no ribbons, medals or trophies for what you did on the trail. You deserve them." Mike said. "However, we both know that if the world knew that a blind dog ran in the big race, there would be many problems."

Mike was right. Many people are not dog lovers and think mushing is bad news. I guess they do not look at the smiles on our faces as we race the trails.

I heard Mike get something out of his pocket. Great; another treat I thought.

"You can not see this, but I know you can picture things in your mind." Mike said very softly. "What I have here is a new collar for you. A special collar, for a special dog, a special friend."

"It is gold in color and has green letters on it that spells out RIVERS, LEAD DOG." He continued, "Besides the big ring for hooking up your harness, I added a smaller ring. On the smaller ring, I have attached all of your racing tags and had a special one made up for you. Anyone who meets you and sees all of these racing tags will know that you are a special dog."

The special tag reads, RIVERS, A TRUE CHAMPION.

With that, Mike took off my old collar, and put the new one on me. I never expected this. It felt very good and I was deeply touched that Mike made it for me. This is too much for a simple, country dog, like me.

I started to howl softly into the night. It was my way of expressing my thankfulness for all that has happen to me this past year. Meeting Mike and his family. All the nice people that helped me have my operation. The new home for my buddies and me. The opportunity to run with my teammates in the great race to Nome. I realized that my life has become a great adventure. I started to wonder what other adventures I would share with my Mike and my teammates.

As I rested my head on Mike's knee, he stroked my head. In the distance, we both heard my teammates howling into the night. Yes, it was very peaceful as we sat there. Just the two of us.